# ALONG THE PATH
# OF ENLIGHTENMENT

# Along the Path of Enlightenment

Sheilana Massey, D.D.

Please direct all inquiries to the author at: 3650 South Pointe Circle #205, Laughlin, Nevada 89029

Published by Lost Coast Press
155 Cypress Street
Fort Bragg, CA 95437
800-773-7782
www.cypresshouse.com

ISBN 1-882897-55-2

Publisher's Cataloging-in-Publication
(Provided by Quality Books, Inc.)
Massey, Sheilana.
    Along the path of enlightenment / Sheilana Massey. — 1st ed.
    p.  cm.
    Includes bibliographical references and index.
    LCCN: 00-90594
    ISBN: 1-882897-55-2

    1. Massey, Sheilana--Religion. 2. Spiritual
biography. 3. Spiritual life. 4. Meditation.
5. Self-actualization (Psychology)  I. Title.

    BL73.M37A3 2000          299.93'092
                    QBI00-500132

Design and cover illustration
by Gopa Design & Illustration

Printed in Canada

*Dedicated to every person, event and activity
that has influenced my life — particularly my parents,
Henry and Alice White, and my sons,
Lawrence and Ron Massey.*

# Table of Contents

# Introduction

AFTER PUBLISHING MY FIRST BOOK, *Peace Has No Space for Memories,* readers commented that they would like to know how the material enhanced my life. This book is about my journey into All That Is. It includes personal experiences, questions and responses that surface from that somewhere within my being, and explores personal incidents that have led me to embrace spirituality, rather than religion, as a way of life. Ten meditations are included, since these are quite relevant to the path I am walking.

I recall my feelings about sharing my personal writings with anyone. Who am I to think anyone would want to read them? Of what interest are my responses to anyone? They get their own messages. What good are mine to others? I know not what messages you might find in this book, for every experience is colored and flavored by personal projections, concepts and feelings about what we call God. Perhaps you will be encouraged to awaken your hidden Essence. Included in these pages are steps that stimulated my development as I learned awakening to be an integral aspect of being human. Direct concepts, meditations and exercises are presented to support an inner journey. I have no answers for you; I have only information that has and is still assisting my growth. Consider reading with an intention to be aware of all levels of stimuli personally held within.

Deep responses to life are difficult to write about because there is really nothing to say—yet there is tremendous energy to convey. Words are for the mind to use while one's real energy is connecting to Essence, a quality of Love that intellect can only begin to describe. This is not written to solve anything, but to stimulate each of us into being willing to discover other possibilities for living fully as Beings of God in an expanded realm of Love.

My adventures have led me to embody the perspective that we are multidimensional Beings and that expanded aspects of our personal streams are available to assist us in this life. Messages that were received in response to my musings are presented to you as they were given to me from these evolved, loving *Beings*. Call them Guides, Angels or any other name you feel comfortable using. I sense them as energies of sovereign mastery. When my mind has a question, I can ask for answers or solutions. These messengers bring answers and tremendous encouragement in their unique manner of explanation. Our interaction has been an instrumental influence on my development of Spiritual consciousness. Always, there is momentous energy beyond what is written—joy, tears, laughter, humbleness, reluctance.

We want you to write that we love you and feel your reluctance to move forward with this project. Allow us to support you through any and every fear that surfaces. Know it is with the pleasure of universes we are co-creating this project. Please realize that your writings are available to many more than your voice can ever reach, no matter how many lectures or groups you work with. It is important for you to continue this work. We feel your joy and your hesitation. They are real only within your scope; there is no basis for them in the essence of this creation. [Tears are flowing.] We encourage you to be diligent in its completion. We are showing you the way, seed-ing the concepts through your writing—for you and many others. Please believe in your Self with trust. You are the physical proponent necessary for this creation.

Humanity is birthed as tender, loving *Beings* with the capacity to be caring individuals. There is a 'silent majority' who grow up in nurturing, loving families. You have refrained from sharing your stories due to concern for making others feel bad, or because those people whose caregivers were so abusive might not be able to relate to thoughtful, supportive parents. For some, childhood was exploration, adventure, cuddling and story reading. This reality has been discussed in very few books; your stories have not been re-told. It is time for you to redefine your availability in regard to media sharing. You have great support. ✸

I am in awe of the flow of this energy and the sensitivity in my fingers and my body while typing. I set my intention to engage more frequently. Once it was as if I were tuned in to three radio stations simultaneously. There was so much information about several different topics. One early morning when the energies were particularly strong, I suggested they give me time to eat breakfast before continuing. The following idea surprised me.

Write down the topics so that you can refer to them later. Where we are is totally Now; we cannot return to something that has happened before. You are the one with the memory, with the attributes necessary to live in what you call time. For us to return, (not achievable but the term is the only thing to use), we have to use your dimensional frequencies—thus we 'use' you. It is in this symbiotic relationship of the greater *we* that people tap into 'time' in order to span every dimension, every universe. ✸

Being immersed in this representation of the Light of God feels all-permeating, all-inclusive. Freedom is being able to explore anything and everything that comes up in my consciousness—without attachment. I encourage each of us to attune to our inner knowing before taking anything from outside ourselves as our own experience or belief. Check out everything.

One interesting aspect has been the connected progression of my own transformation. And now this book has manifested—motivated by requests of readers for more inspiration. Included are exercises and meditations that have been powerful for me and for those in the groups I lead. The most productive way to experience the meditations can be to tape them for yourself. Hearing your own voice present the directions can enhance your experience. While taping, use encouraging tones, articulate carefully and speak slowly, knowing as you speak the meditation, you are activating exactly what Spirit has available for you. Schedule your time to create personal space for each meditation—a place of comfort and safety where you will not be interrupted. If you are alone, responses can be either silent or verbal. With others present, it is best for each to have their own silent experience. The symbol ❀ denotes places to insert pauses; more than one symbol indicates a longer pause is needed.

Everyone has the unique ability to experience infinite possibilities—even within the context of a particular event. Ten people at a family dinner each has his or her own interpretation of what is happening. God is the experience no matter what one's mind, training or belief-system conveys. We are unique. We are Divine. Individually or as a group, we are the expression of evolution—from this experience, to this thought, to this action, into another and another. Although I can write about my awareness, only you read it from your uniqueness and accept, reject or rotate the information to fit into your experience. None of us totally enters into any world other than our own. My earth is different from yours. Try as we might we can only be ourselves. And in the total scope of Creation we are One expressing, experiencing the innumerable ways of individual preference. Let's adventure into expanded possibilities beyond the dimensions of daily living, into the holographic Beingness of Source connection—our unique expression of Self.

# 1 Adventure of Curiosity

I'M IN A CONTINUAL ADVENTURE of discovery that includes searching for myself. My childhood was fun. School had its joys and disappointments. Family life proceeded in rhythm with the various societies in which I lived. Through all of this a sense of excitement prevailed. God was real, connected to some innate possibility within myself and everyone and everything. I was, however, an adult before I realized gratitude for my upbringing in Quakerism. Although there were 'shall nots,' the basic spiritual practices were ready made for me. Teachings about the Spirit within preceded my later introduction to doctrines emphasizing external practices of ritual and ceremony.

I vividly recall my mother's statement after she read a draft copy of *Peace Has No Space for Memories*. She lovingly stated she was glad to see I had not forsaken my Quaker Heritage. A warm feeling flowed within my body when I heard those words. I had not thought about if or how these early activities and doctrines were influencing and impacting my reality when I lived in communities without Meetings. One Sunday morning about ten years ago, a minister said something about the mystical origins and concepts of Quakerism: how George Fox had been quite a mystic. Curiosity about this man's seventeenth century ministry was stimulated. The resulting studies deepened my inner exploration. In his life as a peaceable wandering healer, Fox was frequently chastised by the establishment for his unorthodox practices.

There were other religious events that influenced me as a child. Our family went to several services at the church of the lady who helped Mother. Sadie's father was the minister and we had numerous invitations, particularly for special services. Our family of five was always warmly greeted and ushered to the front pew, hampering my seeing what was happening behind me. It was considered impolite to stare or turn around to look. There was wonderful singing in rhythm, with clapping and swaying punctuated by alleluias and amens. Definitely different from Quaker Meeting.

Once I experienced another type of church service when I visited my girlhood friend after she had moved to another town. While attending a junior-high dance, several of us decided to check out a church that adjoined the schoolyard to witness the music and singing we could hear. The church windows gave a good view of a room full of people clapping, singing and moving around. I was intently watching this new sight when a man came out of the church to usher inside those standing near the door. That I ran is an understatement. Suddenly I was conscious of sitting on the school steps—out of breath and shaking. I was concerned for those who were in that building, totally unsure of what might be happening to them. I never found out.

During my freshman year in college, a Billy Graham Crusade was held under a tent not far from the campus. Since there were few restrictions about attending a religious service, permission to go was given quite easily. The singing by both the choir and the hundreds of attendees was inspiring. The congregation was invited to come forth to 'receive the Lord.' Now as I recall the group dynamics of this gathering, I sense the passion exploding through many participants, particularly the ones who followed the pleas to come to the front for further blessing. It would be difficult to deny the Presence brought forth for this 'washing of the Holy Spirit.' I remember feeling a lightness and a strength beyond any previous worship experience. It ignited something in me while, at the same time, I was hesitant to talk about the experience. It was time for me to go inside myself, to open and be with the influx of energy.

My spiritual studies have included many world doctrines and faiths; however, I've spent most of my life with Christianity. Honor for Jesus is joined by the teachings of many world faiths. Every doctrine has its similarities, some profoundly influencing my reality. In my childhood training the concept of God as a 'punisher' was absent, however during my early twenties—in another denomination—I learned there were other Biblical interpretations. I recall a service in which people sang a song about being washed in the blood of Jesus. Why would God want us to do that? I asked how this request could originate from a God of Love? Possibly this belief about fearing the wrath of God even when "God is Love" sets up humanity's *equating love to fear.* How do such concepts relate to the term Father as associated with God? Does it influence our collective regard of the father/authority/judge complex? Is this the cause-and-effect concept in action? Maybe God-The-Father cannot be described in human terms.

In hindsight, I see that to some extent, I accepted numerous limiting concepts during the several years of activity in various religious environments. Then the deeper questioning began—questions I asked others about their ideas, and numerous books I read that gave consideration to a multitude of concepts. I became more interested in internal experiences, something discouraged in many, if not most religious ideologies. My questioning began with, "Is it OK to have my own personal concepts—even if they are different from those expounded by others? Will something happen to me if I 'go against' the establishment by disassociating from interpretations they consider normal? Is there anyone else out there with such questions?"

The physical aspect of my adventurous life took me to new

locations, too. I was being unconsciously led by my intention for discovery. People appeared who willingly engaged in discussions of other philosophies. A level of excitement surfaced. And was I really conscious of what was happening? Not always. I responded to the energy of my questions and internal leadership. Every now and then a feeling of realness surfaced; then these happened more frequently. Excitement was becoming conscious. I felt a vitality as I re-connected to deeper spiritual truths, to the Spirit within that expanded my Being.

How did I get so far away? Curiosity was always a part of my childhood. When I went to school my investigative nature was thwarted. I talked of things I knew—the fairies my mother showed me living under the blooming maypops beside the creek; angels that flew through my room at night; the toads, butterflies, creeks and creatures that lived under the sand at the ocean—all the exciting things of nature. Classmates ridiculed me, discounted my reality and called me a liar. In my childhood way, I felt hurt and left out. These feelings evolved into a belief that I had nothing important to say, and that what I knew didn't make any difference to anyone. To counteract this tendency, in high school I became a public speaker, singer and actress. I forced myself to learn social conversation so that I would fit in.

In the past ten years these old patterns have been shown to me as a circle spinning in a flat band. Expanded awareness and my altered perception turned this stuck energy just slightly, like turning a doorknob. An opening was created allowing the circle to become a spiral of energy. I was returning to the freedom of my childhood. There is truth to what I feel, think, believe and know.

Twenty years ago someone I respected said God was too busy to deal with everyday details—that He was present only in big happenings. Then I was exposed to the Eastern philosophy about Jesus being 'just a man'—though more holy than the average human. Several years ago my search brought me a book subscribing to the "I am God"[1] concept, which stimulated my desire to consider, sort through, accept, reject or incorporate new ideas, even if only for a few days. This search has led me into many adventures—exciting though at times questionable. Greater awareness surfaced during a ministerial class in 1993 as memories of those formative years surfaced with "we've known this all along." My personal awareness has accelerated to include a more peaceful acceptance of circumstances. By expanding into who we truly are, we explore the spiral of Oneness of all Creation as a reality in life. This changes the energy of perceiving events as 'problems,' thus uncovering underlying truths that can move us into lovingly accepting every experience as a learning situation.

To uncover your own concealed conclusions, consider the following statements. Notice personal ideas that correspond either in agreement or dispute. Be aware of any reactions and their body locations, those that feel good and any that create contraction. You could choose to write them down for later consideration.

Recall your earliest experience with really knowing God. Maybe it included dedicating your life to God.

Recall the feelings associated with the experience.

What has happened in your life since then?

Do you feel fulfilled?

How do you include God within yourself, within everyone and everything?

You are the temple of the living God; "...for ye are the temple of the living God...." (2 Corinthians 6:16)

Jesus said "In my Father's house are many mansions."
(John 14:2)

As individuated parts of God we are to keep our 'house' clean.

And assist everything and everyone in keeping their temples in order.

Cleaning is not a process of sitting on the throne, seeing the fungus, saying 'be gone' or to 'hire someone else to do the job.'

To get to the core, the cause, we must be willing to move the furniture.

The work must be done by me!

Do you feel there is a mystery to healing?

Jesus said "Greater works than these shall ye do..."
( John 14:12 (

What can we do to employ such powers?

Jesus told those He healed to do something—the leper had to "pick up his bed and walk."

What a challenge for the man.

The lady who 'touched the hem' of His garment had to take herself to where He was.

Her neighbor, doctor, priest couldn't do the healing for her.

Pain tells us there is something, some place that is not filled with Love, with Light.

How much God Force healing can come into our 'mansions' right now?

Are we ready for a powerful experience?

It is our I Am Presence that guides us into clearing our personal mansion.

We decide when to open the doors. ✺

ADVENTURE AND CURIOSITY are natural aspects of your Beingness. Most humans have put these attributes on hold or squelched them altogether. Think of what it takes to open yourself to any idea that is foreign to your up-until-now experience. You can be receptive to newness, something beyond what you already know. Sparks of curiosity light the fire of adventure. You could delve into something so new that the end result will be the manifestation of a totally new product or idea. You might expand a known premise to clarify its existential meaning. Whatever brings your interest into excitement—this is your adventure. Going to places you have never been, seeing some mountain from another angle, painting a picture from your mind's eye, discovering some internal communication. Individualized curiosity is this attribute that continually pushes the edges, the known boundaries.

Awaken your inquisitiveness and become conscious carriers of the marvels of investigative imagination. Notice how these qualities presently express in your lives. No one ever turns off all the switches; there are always areas of adventure. If you suddenly become aware of a scent beyond what is normal, do you not begin to use this imagination to 'sniff' out the source of the smell? Many times this proves to avert some tragedy. Other times it leads you into a new place of adventure such as a bakery or flower shop. It can resurrect a memory from the past, suggesting re-examination of this memory to incorporate it within your consciousness in a new way. You have experiences of thinking of someone, calling them to discover an individual sharing or an interlacing idea to explore together. The instantaneous responses from these places of connectedness become springboards for the next adventure. Reconnect your curiosity, follow its leads for deepening personal experiences of Self, of Spirit in your life.

Use curiosity's creative guidance to explore the multiple dimensions of your inherent energy. You are the interpreter for your unique development of Creation—spontaneous expansion. Consciously be in Creation every minute. It is time to begin anew, to move beyond the centuries of past experience, birthing yourselves into a thunder of new vibration for fresh ventures, added vistas and venues. Be a chalice. Open so expansively that Creation, as Its entirety, can be held within. You are everything. You are All That Is. Play with it. Manifest it. *Be It.* ✸

Words of Rick Harlow convey experiences into the depths of self. The artist refers to his adapting to jungle life as "like being an infant again, letting go of a lot of what I thought I knew about the way the world works and opening my perspective to encompass a much wider range of experience."[2] We are exposed to an idea, an experience, a feeling. Our curiosity is urged open to something new—inviting Divine Essence to share Itself as we surrender to Its perfect timing.

It is in assisting ourselves as Light Beings that we transform this world—that we enable Peace on Earth to be reality. I am grateful for and honor every person and every experience of my life for being an active part of this creation called *me*. Through loving myself enough to *do* for me, this enlivening energy transfers to others. The power of Light is never diminished. Asking for more is asking ourselves to be aware of barriers, fogs, obstacles and habits that are presently unconscious of our Light. The desire of Source is that we take in all we can, that we *be* Source. We tap into this energetic to intensify this inherent Light in us—and we become One. The resulting joy of the moment alters the adventures of everyone within the experience—physically and energetically. "And God said, 'Let there be Light.'"[3]

# 2  Flow of Ordination

❧ I am aware of a brilliant oval of light six feet or so from my body. I relax into its power, aware of infiltration as though minute multicolored flecks were coming towards me. It is as if being showered with sparkles of Light, layering over and infiltrating everything. They create sensations upon my skin and continue their gentle descent until I am enveloped. I sense me as a spiraling fleck flowing and undulating within the midst of this shower. I move into an expanse of everything and no thing, a stabilizer, a balance between here and there, up and down, in and out. A very intimate feeling spirals through me creating marvelous sensate pulses, interacting particularly with my heart. There is peace and joy with tremendous Love energy without regard to what, when or where. This is All There Is—Infinity. And it surrounds and includes All. ❧

JESUS HAS WALKED WITH ME; He's talked to me—through tapes, through himself and today, through *Joshua*,[4] an audio book I have been listening to. Jesus has been the trees lying on the beach—weathered, whitened, washed pieces of wood. He's been the smiles of friends and people I have never met before—the waitress, the gentleman pumping gas. He's been the sound of children having fun on the ferry. He's in the green of trees as I drive over the hills. Today He is not a man. He's an Energetic, a *Beingness* of All That Is, so precious, so filling and nourishing it brings a flow tears. When one is ready for that step, the Spirit of personal ordination is embodied by each of us. Ordination manifests as an influx of energy far greater than anything known in the past as an incorporation of physicality and Spirit.

This present energy is more tangible, more stable, incorporated more consciously into my entire *being* than any previous initiation transmission. And, I don't know what 'it' is. I'm learning through these experiences, understanding about possibilities that might occur. And yet at this moment all is possibility. I accept that this will change my way of being with people because it's changing the way I am with myself. And I don't know what that's going to look like. There is a freedom within while at the same time there's an obligation. The obligation may be to merely be in this place and open myself to this expansive energy that's available for everyone. In opening up this way, I am free, a freedom— I don't have words for this. Knowingness is the only word representation that seems to connect.

This ordination is an experience of knowing that everything Is; everything is happening just exactly the way it must. This brings freedom from any feeling about the necessity to change anything, away from attempts to have things different than they are right now. It's an acceptance that is… there aren't words…. It's a place of recognition, freely riding the energy, undulating, spiraling with it. It is in flow with the rhythm—there it is—in flow with the rhythm of Creation. *Wheee! In flow with the rhythm of Creation.*

I want to feel this … to feel the energetics of *In flow with the rhythm of Creation.* The mind jumps in to analyze, to categorize. I hear laughter. It is sort of funny. The mind wants to look at it, to really do something with it, to bring 'meaning' to the statement, the words, rather than just being in the flow, being in the feeling of this. So quick to jump in. I'm loosening the mental and opening again just to the feeling. *Being* in the flow of Creation in this moment.

So let me keep my mind busy while I feel this. (The dialogue of my mind.) I am driving down the highway in western Oregon. It's a beautiful sunny morning. The temperature is cool but not cold, invigorating. I have spent time with beauty—people and places. I think of others and know things are happening for them without me. I don't have to be in their lives, be with them; they don't have to be with me. Each of us is our own independent self while we also relate. And in that time frame we share with one another supporting ourselves and others from where we are. It brings a real acceptance of flow. Each of us is flowing perfectly in the moment.

Part of me hears this message, "*Yes, yes. Just be with this. We are with you. Continue what we are doing.*"

Then questions come up. "How can this work in everyday life? Is being in this space becoming separate from the world?" No. That's just the mind, the ego/personality booming in with, "How would the world operate if everyone felt this way? If no one takes initiative?"

THOSE LOGISTICS are beyond your imagination. It is happening. And yes, it will be a new experience. As people gain awareness of their own sovereignty, they become aware of freedom and their personal space of flow in the rhythm of Creation. So, you learn to be in this space individually and then expand it into two and three and ten of you, and two organizations and seven organizations. Just as you are aware that the principal of the masses works in everything, this will also come to pass. Right at this moment you really do not have a concept on which to base this; here and there in small areas of civilization there are a few working examples. It takes more people aware of the possibility, being ready to explore expanded dimensions of personal reality. Be assured, this is happening. ✹

These recent experiences have moved me through portals beyond my imagination. Opening to this rhythm of energy is a beautiful experience. The portal of Jesus 'over came' me, washing away so many old patterns. When I welcome Him into my presence and accept I am in His presence, new understandings of what is possible are available. This is not a flippant remark, but a knowing, an understanding beyond what has been previously. It is within living a different way—just what this will look like is not clear. One way I know includes supporting others in their growth, thus supporting myself. No one has to do anything any differently. *Freedom* is the primary key—love supporting us through whatever we decide to explore, without judgment or censoring. Each does it her/his way and yet by using the sustenance that comes from Christ Love, doors open beyond anyone's expectation, enabling totally experiencing that lesson and moving on into a new alignment with love.

So what was real for me yesterday and today is that Jesus appears in a multitude of ways—through words of others, through the forest, beaches and the sea and as the container that holds the ocean. He comes through the elements of weather, sunshine and breezes. Through the birds and animals, through footprints in the sand, the blackberries I picked and ate. I am a container to be filled by all forms of His Presence. The energetics of this bond are powerful, a focus connecting all aspects of life—conscious or not. This energy is where true healing occurs. When in this space I heal myself and I can send it to others for them to use as they choose. In opening to this energy miraculous things happen without mindful concentration. There may be little conscious realization of the healing process. Avoid any tendency to stop short of completion. We experience many lessons and when completed we've continued to carry the empty sack. It is important to stay in the progression of healing until the container has entirely dissolved or transformed.

The 'doing' comes from a place of self-connection to love that is reflected to us as it is within ourselves. We may notice struggle going on between the personality that knows not and the divine that is love. And when we're in the space of love, the 'I Am' will always see itself in every thing. The mirror is always there even when clouded by personality actions. The secret is to look through the clouds, going to what is truly present. It is divine union with every aspect of God, All That Is. The greater connection we have to this divinity the more we realize that everything any of us is experiencing is our Soul attempting to clear the clouds presented by the personality. As we move through processes of entanglement, unwinding, regrouping into our personal power, we can then see the truth of Godliness in ourselves and others. The circle that was looping round and round becomes a spiral of energy that envelops the next phase of enlightenment. We can intend to live the Spirit-directed flow of this present creation.

Within me Godness flows, permeates and spreads out like water. Nothing escapes this Essence of the Sea of God. It floods. It infiltrates into other beings, lighting sparks in their containers, instigating movement. It spirals, becomes a fountain, like a waterspout. From endless reservoirs integrally filled with God come sparkles—energies of Light. A sea of moving brilliance. As we embody our totality filled with God Essence the contents overflow to surround others in these life sparkles. Once started, no individual can stop it. I experience the progression stabilizing within myself in the excitement of this transmission. To say this is ecstasy is an understatement. Words don't work.

# 3 Considering Freedom

ANY COMMITMENT to live in this moment immediately opens avenues to being conscious of the present—as a leaf on a tree until some force of nature takes it into flight. Or we are free as birds and butterflies, being present and moving—energy permeating rather than pushing. Here is a personal experience that occurred while I was being present in relaxation, sitting in an open shelter during a warm, gentle rain.

꩜ I am a droplet of water, moving, falling free. There is no other sensation. I am within a multitude of other energies, sounds and sensations. I come in contact with something that alters the motion, interrupts falling. Now I am in relationship with a surface. Movement continues in a different way; I slide across this plane of leaf. Evaporation might happen right here. The cycle would begin again.

In this moment other energies such as I also gather on this surface. We unite in this place until our weight tips the leaf and we again free fall—to another surface—and another and another. Perhaps on our journey we land in a body of our own kind, to become a drop in a bucket or a particle of ocean. It's possible to collide with a windshield to be swished aside. Or to be caught in the hand of a child. ✦

Each raindrop has an individual existence while being part of the whole storm, creating life in the moment without thought, plan, expectation, judgment. There are so many possibilities for continuation as specks of energy. Some droplets become nourishment for plants and animals, some creeks or seas. Consider the 'life span' of any particle of water. I might be a drink for a bird, support for a rice field, steam from a kettle or home to a host of other life forms. Each droplet moves though cycles of numerous realities—from one to another *freely*.

I wonder how it would be for us to be who we are in our totality? To relate to our world as a droplet of water, cycling through every possible reality? As part of a greater whole, splashed out of this body into another scenario? Can we move so freely and maintain our entelechial consciousness? Can we be an individual flower of humanity, connected and part of the whole—in integrity, truth, words, actions and expressions?

One day I had some awareness concerning why I am comfortable being separate—related to being *free*—away from anyone's control. I am so comfortable being 'out there' close to Source and other non-physical Beings—so sovereign, without separation. At some point I realized that the sense of separation is only on this plane, that the culprit is human thought. Here on earth freedom can be restricted so quickly, so completely. My mind/ego says if I really open myself to the complete loving of any human, I will lose freedom since whomever would expect something from this love. I felt the imprisonment, the restrictions of human interaction. There was a knowing that the release of this belief was the next step. My choice was to work through the tangle, accepting that an even greater freedom is beyond. To experience this required my letting go of any desire and choose total God direction—total compassion that comes from immense love for everything. I grounded my intention to go through this into the next state of bliss.

While being lovingly supported by a friend, I chose to look at my desire to be free, to be who I am in the moment—without feeling abandoned. I touched into other people who feel less than free. My fear of absolute freedom contained not being seen or included, thus being ignored. My intellect knew this was irrational, however, the feelings persisted. I began to delve into freedom, freedom to go anywhere, do anything. Mentally I realized I already have this. I have complete freedom to do whatever I want, travel anywhere I choose. I have accepted that I can do this alone. Part of me was wary of letting this present status go. Another part wanted someone else to enjoy these things with me. And yet with all of this mental awareness, resolution did not occur; the feelings I started with persisted.

While moving through layer after layer, I began to feel a fear associated with exalted freedom, fear of freedom where there is nothing to do, nothing to be. It was as though there were no reason for existence. Why be? I felt loneliness within true freedom. Abject terror surfaced; fear of this loneliness of being everything. My mind went into responsibility—entering into faultfinding, imperfection, less than, all aspects of 'not good enough.'

As I stayed with this terror, watching my mind and opening my emotions, I experienced that within my interpretation of freedom there was no one with whom to share the inevitable sovereignty that exists. I really felt the aloneness of God when in the beginning It contained Itself as all there was. I understood Creation as an awesomely passionate energy interacting with Itself. Words do not adequately express what happened. Tears and harmonic tones flowed. I felt my heart expand, filling with a new energy. The process moved me very consciously into total acceptance of myself as God, as a Creator. I cried at the realization that all of us are already in that space, cried that we all become aware in our own lives. I really got that I am All That Is.

I am, you are, we are the Face of God—the hands, ears, eyes of God. All is in perfection, free and good. Inherent Goodness flows into freedom and continues into the awesome-ness of Totality, The One. Exhilarating energy flowed freely, a spiral of Light moving in and through my *Being*. Shivers of ecstasy ran throughout my physical body as I moved with these energies of freedom without context, reason or definition.

My friend was very present, so loving and supporting from her Heart Essence, thus opening her energy to feel her perception of what was occurring for me. Individually each of us experienced this soaring for the duration of the transmission with complete creative connection.

My mind thought it had freedom's concepts down pat. I've talked about them, explained and expounded upon them. I taught and wrote about ideas that have assisted others with greater freedom and joy in their lives. This experience was way beyond those mental constructs. Experiencing educates the knowing. What I had previously said from my mind were words that had prepared me for the actuality of total expression—feeling, thoughts, truth of the moment enveloped in instantaneous Essence. I realized I've embodied the Essence presented in the first book I wrote. I accepted my healership when I received the information included in the chapters about God and Transition.[5] This particular freedom experience was more than a connection to HigherSelf—it was all the way to God. The message was clear, "You are living the book." It was in the realm of owning who I am while knowing who you are. This happened in the depths of my Soul, my Soul's realization of Its totality. It changed the way I see with my physical eyes; it changed my perceptions; it changed my life.

The experiences over the following forty-eight hours were quite interesting. There was an embodied realization that we do everything *just for the experience*. It makes no difference what we do when—only that we be aware of *our* experience in each situation—how we engage with others, share, exchange, react, judge or ignore. Freedom is our experience in the moment, the ultimate available reality, free from conditions, material desires, purpose—even pleasure. My choice reflects how I allow my emotions and thoughts to interrupt my freedom to be the Creator of my every moment. While I am in this awareness (certainly not all the time), things that could be classified as interruptive or complicated are just an opportunity to experience whatever interchange is taking place now. I don't have choice in how others respond to me, only in how I interact with the situation that is presenting itself. I can be argumentative or confrontational. Or I can be very present in the moment, ignoring thoughts about similar situations from the past or thoughts that project into the future.

Many times I'm acutely aware of being in the moment for the experience—with no expectation or regard for the outcome. Freedom. Nothing seems to bother me; everyone does what they need to do for whatever reason. Politeness carries through each encounter. Compassion is ever present. The flow is gentle, easy and productive for all concerned. From these happenings new pathways of knowing are formed, not to think about, but to assemble old material to expand my awareness. I have never done what I am now doing in this particular way. How is it to let things occur without attachment to any outcome? When I am consciously aware of in-the-moment experience, each becomes a new equation for life's situations. I visited a close friend two days after one of these adventures. She wanted to know what had happened to me, saying that I looked and talked differently. I do know I felt different. Life is at the surface of me, not pushed back behind what needs to be done.

EVERY EXPERIENCE is an opportunity for your Self/ Soul/God connection to express. You can choose to do it as done in the past (a learned response) or you can choose to venture into the moment differently. It is your freedom to choose which aspect of your multidimensional person engages with whatever is occurring. When you use the personality, your actions will be similar to what has been done before. If you use your Soul perspective, the engagement will be based on encoded Spirit principles. When you open to the freedom of God expressing, everything is different—your thoughts, your feelings, the outcomes and responses. In fact, many times other people in the interaction become confused as to what to do, since when you are connecting to God/Creator energies, there is such peace that any interaction resounds from a new place. It is as if everyone concerned were blending from a different perspective. Confusion may surface because others are mentally unaware of the energy source that is guiding the moments. Anyone who is aware of where their energy connection lies, realizes they are not in control and yet, there are no ruffled feathers. Smooth is the action. This does not come from an ungrounded space; it is very grounded—the only way to really connect to your God center. Some call this letting go, detachment, surrender.

All the while the Essence of the highest creation possible is manifesting, ungluing the old patterns that have been often repeated and ingrained within the personality structure. Feel this: *I can let go and 'let God' to the extent that I am claiming my Godhood.* Everything is new in the moment. Live this way. Become instantaneous creators. Claim your Divine heritage. Be the moment. ✹

Being immersed in the Light of God is all permeating, all-inclusive. There are no strings attached to anything, no going anywhere. There is freedom for all expressions, adventures, experiences, inventions, and/or imaginings. Freedom is being able to explore anything and everything that comes up in my consciousness—without attachments. Judgments and criticism come from thinking one knows the 'right' way. There is only the way—for you—for me—for us—for each and every one. And presently I can find no thing on earth that is totally free. Can we truly know freedom?

WHEN ONE MOVES into absolute freedom, there are no boundaries; there is nothing pushing, nothing to push against or for. There is freedom within the containment of a tree in that the tree *is*. Looking from your human self, a tree has no decisions to make; it gets water when its roots are healthy; it absorbs sunshine when its leaves and/or branches are absorbing. There is no exertion. Animals, birds, insects have a more roving freedom in that they can move about. Their biological makeup is such that they must do something physical to obtain food. Free from a past or future, a natural course of life programmed within them. Add humans to this list—the only ones who seem to let an apparent need for control of their environment direct their lives. Which is the most free? Trees cannot decide to move to the next forest. Animals, birds waste no time wondering where they will be next year. Humans can move anywhere, can be on the other side of the planet within hours. And what about water and dirt, rocks, sticks and stones? They change physical proportions, they move with some unseen force from this form to that. Is this freedom?

You allow your mental and emotional capabilities to say you are free "*if*...." You can get up when you want to, eat when you're hungry, go see another person, another locality; you can say anything that comes to mind, even be physically active with others. Is this Freedom?

All the above are contained within certain parameters, boundaries that embody certain functions appropriate to the species. Nothing alters these basic parameters, which allows the *Being* life as it is known on earth. When a tree's bark is punctured, either the bark scars itself to close the wound or it produces additional growth creating a protruding scab. If you didn't have skin would you 'run' out of yourselves all over the place? You know any abrasion produces bleeding and that biological attributes close the laceration. It seems there is no way to be as free as water, to fall freely, to flow here or there, to evaporate into the atmosphere, to be held and released. Eventually your physical body becomes as a stick on the forest floor, mutating from its physical properties to mulch, to dirt. So what is there to be free?

Freedom has no container, i.e. physicality. It has no boundaries, i.e. riverbank. It continually moves beyond. Freedom is more than having money to purchase a plane ticket to Timbuktu. More than having all the ice cream one can eat. Freedom has no reason for curfews, for plans. What does it take for you to really feel the possibilities of total freedom? Can you stretch your imagination enough to touch this for just an instant? ✸

When I explored this concept I connected to the earlier terror—that place where there was nothing to do, nothing to see, nothing to be. It was as if I am nothing—beyond want, desire, even intention. It was as if I were everything, and everything was doing exactly what was necessary to do without any interference or assistance from me. I could drop in on any scene anywhere; no one cared whether I was there or not. I had no influence on what was happening; everything was in motion beyond my influence. So who am I?

The terror of not really knowing who I am lasted several minutes. Then a voice asked, "What brings you pleasure?" This set me back, out of freedom. Are decisions part of freedom? The prison of the mind? What is the truth? I recalled a statement credited to Brian O'Leary about how the truth will set us free, but first it will piss us off. Again I went into freedom. More questions surfaced. Where would it lead? Would it go anywhere? Is there anything other than this? Could freedom just be—without constructs? Not that the mind can imagine. In spite of the questioning mind, I felt freedom. And I don't know words to express this feeling. I wonder how, or if, one can stay in this place twenty-four hours a day.

YOU ARE IN THAT FREEDOM *only* when you are in the present moment of all possibility. This takes practice, a willingness to be something you are not used to being. The key isw awareness of what is every moment. Not what just happened or what you are going to do when you finish this. In fact, there is no finishing. *You Are.* In every moment is all possibility. The movement into absolute freedom is solitary; each must come into this space on his own.

It is this freedom that does create your universe, your encounters. Challenges take form when one expresses the momentary truth and another hears this as having something to do with him/herself. Human conditioning has produced so many scars to your psyche. As one person shares his truth, the listener's judgment is activated and the sparks begin to fly. When this happens, stop! Come back out of reaction into personal awareness with intention to realize what has happened. Some part of your container is either closed or imploded. The contraction is detrimental. Transform it or carry this energy into the future. You can live this freedom. The sovereign You only uses the body as your body uses a house. It is a structure for experiences. You are free. Come to know yourself as free to experience God. This is freedom, the Essence of your life. ❀

# 4 Meditation to Activate HigherSelf Awareness

THIS MEDITATION is to activate awareness of your HigherSelf, that inner voice that we sometimes notice. HigherSelf has always been part of us, yet we usually ignore this Presence. I see this aspect of us as the energetic conductor of our Soul to human connection, holding a loving space of compassion and guidance for our humanity.

We ask for a unique signal to validate us when we are listening to our HigherSelf instead of our ego/personality or some other being not connected to our Soul. Frequent signals are tingles in certain body parts, shivers, movement of a finger or the head, a ringing in the ears, hearing or knowing a word or phrase. My first conscious connection twenty years ago was signaled by a tingling at the tip of my nose. This has expanded into most of my body, sometimes stronger in various parts like nose, lips, fingers or toes.

Since there is power in purposeful togetherness, inviting another person to experience this with you will support both of you. It is helpful to repeat this meditation three times in succession with a short pause between to mentally register what happened. Continued practice will strengthen the connection. Listen for any messages, watch for pictures or movement. Journaling is a great way to deepen the experience.

See the Introduction, page 6, for additional ideas pertaining to taping the meditations. Always follow your guidance.

꙰

Sit comfortably, allowing your body to relax. ❀

Breathe out any tension, any concerns, as your body continues to relax. ❀

Ask your personal Angels and Guides, the Archangels and Masters to be present. ❀

Request any other higher dimensional Beings you want to be present as well. ❀

Use your breath to continue deepening this relaxation. ❀

Set your intention to open your imagination to your HigherSelf. ❀ ❀

If you have experienced your HigherSelf previously, you can ask that this energy connection be intensified. ❀

Be aware of your heart area, the whole chest front and back. ❀

Breathe deeply into this heart place. ❀

Now take your attention to Earth; to a location where you feel safe and supported. ❀ ❀

If one does not come to mind, use your imagination to create a pleasant Earth-place of comfort and safety. ❀

Breathe into this Earth place, connecting your heart to Earth. ❀

Notice how any remaining tension leaves as you feel safe and secure. ❀

Move your attention to your connection to Soul. Just allow this awareness to happen without direction. ❀ ❀

Ask your HigherSelf to be very present.  ❁

Request your HigherSelf to give you a signal;  ❁

It may be a body sensation, a tone, a word. However this happens is perfect.  ❁

Be attentive for this inner voice and its signal.  ❁

If you are unclear, repeat your request.  ❁

Thank your HigherSelf for assisting you to know Its signal.  ❁

Ask if there is a message for you.  ❁ ❁

Listen and watch carefully. It may appear as a color, an object, a feeling or a knowing.  ❁

If you have questions, ask and listen for answers.  ❁ ❁

Pay attention to every sensation and/or thought.  ❁

Thank your HigherSelf for this assistance.  ❁

Set your intention to become more aware of this part of yourself.  ❁ ❁

Ask your mind to retain all that has happened.  ❁

Breathe from your heart into Earth and back to your heart.  ❁ ❁

Bring your attention now to your physical body, noticing all feelings and sensations.  ❁

Take a couple of deep breaths, returning your attention to your body position and support.  ❁

Slowly and gently move the fingers, feet, legs; begin to stretch.  ❁

Open your eyes and be aware of your surroundings, gradually becoming totally conscious of where you are and how you feel. ❀❀ ✿

Be aware of what you have experienced.
You might want to journal this encounter to anchor it more fully.

# 5 My Particular Path

THE WHOLE CONCEPT of the term healing came into perspective when I read one of Dr. Bernie Siegel's[6] books years ago. Until that time, my thoughts related to the usual medical terminology about disease. During and after reading the book, many familiarities formerly 'tucked away' began to surface. My internal questioning of what could be accomplished expanded. This continues today, from the first lessons about laying on of hands to connecting with aspects beyond the physical, the GodForce energy that comes through me. This has been a powerful personal process, one that continually evolves. Concepts and experiences grow upon one another, expanding present awareness. I use what I have while being open for what is to come.

Since consciously beginning the path of a healing ministry in the seventies, several challenges with being physically ill have occurred. I experienced areas of the medical community heretofore unknown to me. From my present perspective I see that the decisions I made then would now be different. I am convinced that healing is far beyond the physical, interlaced in our words and actions, emotions, thoughts and ideas. Disease is a result of energetic interactions that can be changed prior to manifestation in physical reality.

I began studying various types of healing modalities, practicing these with myself and others—hands-on healing, inner child, hypnotherapy, neuro-linguistic programming, techniques of est and Silva Mind Control. My studies continued to certification levels in several of these fields. Even with these, there were instances when some form of the old interchange resurfaced. Why did we have to go into the same place over and over? What's with these healing methods? Introduction to the healing properties of 'past' life awareness brought some answers. Particular characteristics seemed not to begin in this lifetime. Methods of taking the mind into any of these patterns and, with mind, releasing them seemed logical and practical. Now I thought everything could be healed. This method didn't work in some circumstances either. There seemed to be stubborn patterns that hung on. What was going on? Dr. Carl Symington[7] was having wonderful results in his Texas clinic. And I had experienced his visualization and meditation principles with very positive results while diligently working on my own healing in 1988. Yet I still wondered if physical healing was even possible. Possibly I hadn't done anything, maybe the lab tests were incorrect. Perhaps there were no abnormal cells to begin with or that 'it' was still there.

Before this, in 1980, I was hospitalized with an infection the doctors couldn't identify until tests were run. The numerous diagnostic tests took four days while my fever ran very high, creating considerable concern for my life. I was so uncomfortable that on the fifth night I vented my anger toward the doctor who was lovingly caring for me. For about thirty minutes I ranted and raved about the lack of my progress, even though they finally knew the cause. The next morning my fever was near normal. I felt remorse over my outburst, apologizing to the physician. I later realized that my holding this anger buildup was also holding the germ within my system, creating a fever to burn away the dross. The responsible patterns are now obvious when I consider all that was going on in my life at that time. Because of an unexpected and painful divorce, I was alone for the first time with deep concerns and fear about my survival and abilities.

One other learning with this incident had to do with letting my family and loved ones know I was ill. With the exception of one son who lived nearby, I didn't want to 'bother' anyone. What could those who lived hundreds of miles away do? Why worry my loving parents? My decision robbed them of the opportunity to share their love, concern and prayers.

Eleven years after this incident, I attended Dr. Robert T. Jaffe's[8] presentation of energy healing concepts based on his professional practice with patients. Aha! This is the next step! Within the first ten minutes of his lecture I decided to study with him through any and all classes. This commitment continued through graduation from this energy healing school to becoming a staff member, a teacher, and workshop leader. It was a fascinating and wonderful exploration igniting tremendous growth for me.

All the concepts of these various teachers and modalities have meshed to strengthen me and my awareness of numerous possibilities. I now work at deeper levels within myself, acknowledging the cohesiveness of all techniques when used with the direction of HigherSelf. My background of various modalities is helpful in assisting clients with differing modes of living to access their deeper truth. Some need mind stimulation, others process best within a modality that invites feelings and sensations to surface. Many clients are ready to acknowledge their Source connection and use this energy to heal issues presented. Sometimes our actions look like love and joy, other times like anger or fear. Whatever they look like they are all expressions of God. It behooves all of us to connect our personal endeavors with Spirit, opening our hearts to bring Divine Love into reality.

When intentional connection to Spirit, Heart and Awareness is used, healing can track to the core of discomfort. From this core we can examine the conditions to discover the energy's original intention, and make conscious decisions as to our need for this interaction in present-day activities. The resulting transformation changes thoughts and behavior patterns. A phenomenon known as the Soul Merge is frequently a result of a powerful healing experience. It is an exercise of *being*—an anchoring of consciousness and Source into physical reality. With this foundation infusions of Light/Love become more frequent. As we clear unproductive debris from our fields these transmissions become quite powerful and assist in creating definite changes in everyday life.

The realization of such probabilities has opened another world for me, another place of commitment to this planet and to the Source of my *Being,* the I Am, God. The culmination so far is a space of allowing—accepting what is present now with fewer judgments or expectations about what is coming next. I accept myself and others 'as is,' thereby recognizing the Oneness of all.

LIVING ON EARTH in any society conditions one's mind to perceive in particular ways—pictures, sounds, colors and smells. You are taught that these physical perceptions are reality, that there is no other. As children you were denied your 'imaginary playmates.' You learned only adult reality was acceptable and as teenagers most of you rebelled in some manner. There are things going on around one all the time that are clairvoyantly visible. Everyone can see this way. The first step to seeing beyond physical eyes is to accept that you do sense other vibrations, even when the mind denies the possibility of anything other than physical form. Then one can begin to experience scenes during waking time similar to seeing in the dream state.

❧

Begin developing your perception with eyes closed, using the eyelids as a viewing screen.

Relax into self, opening permission to be shown something familiar such as your car.

Then move to something that is not physical—Angels or
Guides are a good place to start.

Accept whatever picture comes.

Awaken to this 'dream' state. It is yours to enjoy. All cells
of one body, one Earth. It is up to you to connect. ℘

The progression of my knowledge of healing continues to
serve myself and those with whom I am working. One idea that
I have used and taught for years comes from the Angelic Kingdom. Their availability is immediate when assistance is requested, always willing to minister to humanity with loving support.
Several clients have had very profound results using the method
of asking one or more Angels to attend to someone with whom
the client is having difficulty. (The next chapter will assist your
conscious connection to these *Beings*.)

For example, one client was assigned a new secretary who felt
she knew a more efficient way to perform office tasks. Since
Tammy didn't like changes she rejected all suggestions. Nita did-
n't want to give in to her new boss. She thought Tammy should
not dictate how secretarial duties should be done. I suggested
that in conjunction with her HigherSelf, Tammy ask two angels
to be with Nita and that when she saw her she remember that
both angels were present. Several days later Tammy called to
share her insights. She said that when Nita approached, she saw
the angels over the secretary's shoulders. Immediately after this
their relationship changed. Tammy's concept of Nita and her job
attributes altered. The office was much more efficient and everyone was happier. (No real names are used here.)

Another client had major changes in the interactions with her
birth family. Laura felt isolated and betrayed by her mother and

several siblings. About three months after asking for angelic assistance she received a warm letter from a brother and a sister. During the next six months family members began interacting with consideration for one another's realities. These dramatic changes occurred in the relationships without the birth family's conscious knowledge of Laura's request for angelic assistance. Since any difficulty with others is our personal creation, our thoughts and emotions about the issue must change for our reality to be altered. We can use the awareness of angelic assistance as a powerful, co-creative tool for transformation of sensitive situations.

Another aspect of co-creation is through 'distance' healing. The effectiveness has expanded with my deepening commitment to personal spiritual growth. Acknowledging our Oneness creates a strong desire to assist others. Through frequent use of intention, prayer and Angels, the people on whom I am focusing Spirit's energies receive their own miracles. An opening seems to be created for the person's Soul to bring through important information to be used in their personal awareness. The inner connectivity of all things, however experienced, is a context of Soul. On whatever plane we may be in the moment, I know that all is in alignment, a spiral of evolving consciousness.

It is never my intention to fix anyone else. Those who are involved with me for manipulative reasons leave rather quickly because my choice is to teach self-empowerment. In joyful fascination I watch the growth of clients and students who have been with me for several years and their personal acceptance of the Spirit of Healing. As with myself, they have opened a heightened awareness of self-love, while consciousness evolves beyond antiquated beliefs. Layer by layer they recognize old patterns, replacing them with new choices for self-acceptance. As we do this for ourselves, we view our behavior and that of others with less judgment and more compassion.

Combining healing fundamentals with the energetics of

verbalization is another vital tool. It has a twofold reward—it utilizes the left brain capabilities, keeping the mind focused on the proceedings rather than on 'what ifs.' It also enhances the process with the energy of sound. Thoughts seem to think differently than they talk. Often clarity is instantaneous when we give our thoughts voice. Healing occurs faster and more completely when all of our facilities are used—including our ability to share all facets of the process verbally.

When I was studying inner-child facilitation the teachers kept insisting I connect with some traumatic childhood experience. I now know that HigherSelf was directing, even if this wasn't acknowledged. I described the scene of a piano recital at the age of eight or nine. I played after my best girlfriend had received a large bouquet of flowers after her performance. The child me was very disappointed when I didn't receive flowers also. In reviewing this scene, I felt my inner-child's anguish and questioning about playing good enough. The child me still didn't understand, but as I perceived the experience through my adult eyes I saw that Barbara's father sent flowers since he was unable to be present that night because of his work schedule. My father, mother, sisters and grandparents were in the audience.

These types of scenes are frozen in our memories, influencing our perceptions of incidents in today's life, frequently creating detrimental reactions to present situations. Delving into related emotions in any given situation brings information about repressed feelings that evolve from the core experience, regardless of when it occurred. When the inner-child/children feel safe enough they will share great knowledge of the situation. This awareness leads to transformational healing at a much faster pace.

My healing emphasis opened a natural flow into ministerial studies. I realized my spiritual leadership began many years ago, before I had any conscious knowledge of personal ministry. Benefits include my commitment to Earth and all its inhabitants—not just people. The deepening of my Essence awareness moves through my fields with compassion for every particle of this planet. We are here together in the evolution of Source. That some of the scenes look devastating is part of evolution, a polarity of time, the opposite sides of expression. Turn fear into excitement, flip hate into love, sorrow into joy. Change rigid beliefs about duality; consider the possibility that what is termed negativity is also Source. Gain insight into creation, a space of ultimate compassion—The Oneness of all things.

When I look back over the years since my youngest son went to college, I marvel at the procession of events my Soul has directed me to explore. It's interesting to notice how my choices have built upon each other. Within these experiences I have a greater awareness of who I am, what I can do, and where I have been, giving me confidence about the validity of my path as it unfolds. Perspectives are stimulated, providing incentive to share with others. As I grow, you grow; as you expand, I expand.

Ten years ago I had no idea where I would be today. I choose the path of self-discovery, knowing my spiritual development is a priority for me and I will continue interacting with humanity. As I check with my HigherSelf/Soul guidance, that wiser, more conscious Soul connection assures me that my future is for my optimum growth—as it is for each of us. To me there is loving support for my intention to be involved with experiences and opportunities for healing of all qualities of the planet—Peace on Earth.

# 6 *Infinity and Earth*

WHEN I FIRST HEARD the expression "ground your energies," I was totally innocent of what was being requested. Since then I have learned the importance of connecting our consciousness to this planet and to our physical body as well. It is constructed of earth components that will return to its beginnings. Mainstream Christianity supports Jesus' words: Love your God with all your heart, all your Soul, and with all your mind.[9] There is one more step that completes a circle of energy to totally support our life existence—to be aware of and love our connection to the Earth.

Create steadiness by connecting to Earth even stronger. With this action you broaden your base alignment allowing more of yourself into life. This is the idea of grounding the energies—to bring more of your own energy into you for use in every activity, every feeling, every thought. The movement into your Self is just that—opening, accepting and grounding your creation. This is an important requirement for the success of your intention to be all that you can be.

An important aspect of parenting is to provide children with activities involving dirt, grass, woods, and trees to anchor their *Beingness* to this plane of existence. The strength they develop in their physical bodies comes through grounding. In any type of what you call 'sports' it is meaningful to ground your energy—thus avoiding falls, missteps, tumbles, particularly with indoor activities. This is true regardless of the participants' ages. With outdoor exercise be aware that concrete solidifies most of the necessary components of this earth energy, making it more difficult to absorb enough Earth energy for proper grounding.

Grounding is particularly crucial for people who are experiencing health challenges; exposing them to some type of relationship to earth is vital. Create a nature corner in convalescent rooms; attach a flower to the bed sheet; bring a pet to the bedside. Witness the interaction between children and animals—vitality improves. Add regular exposure to meadows, creeks, vacant lots and parks of urban areas, sunshine and rain. Watch the energy level accelerate. For assistance with chaotic behavior patterns, add meals primarily of root vegetables along with outdoor exercise. Active playing or swimming in natural waters is intensely recuperative.

These elements of healthful living are not just for children. So frequently adults think they outgrow the need to play, to have outdoor activity. It is vital for everyone to participate in the natural habitat they live in. Formal exercise is seen as necessary particularly for vascular health. Just what does the vascular system do for the body? It feeds every minute physical aspect with available earthly nutrients. Without this circulation you would be immobile. And what is the primary connection? Your heart—the seat of Spirit and Earth.

Love your physical body. Love your heart. Love your Soul. Love your life on Earth. ✳

One of the exercises I learned as a student in a healing school is using breath to enhance my Heart/Soul connection—sensing or visualizing the breath in a circular pattern through the heart and wherever Soul is perceived to be. The original pattern of this breath was inhaling from Soul into the back of my heart, exhaling out the front of my heart to Soul. Continuing to do this, I realized I was getting lightheaded. Immediately my HigherSelf told me to also breathe similarly from my heart to the ground under my feet. Instantly I felt an influx of connective energy that surged straight into my heart and spread throughout my body. This was warm, fuzzy and intensely passionate. I became very relaxed, realizing this feeling is totally natural to my physical body, though I had no previous conscious recollection of this.

At some point after my incorporating this technique, my breaths began to expand and connected themselves as if I were breathing an infinity sign—Soul, Heart, Earth, as taught by AlixSandra Parness.[10] For me, the inhale connected from Soul through Heart to Earth; the exhale in reverse. The heart is the crucible, the crossover point of the figure eight.

For me this practice has evolved into using the basic principle in numerous ways, particularly with healing. Remember, this is pure Light working in you. The next chapter is a meditation to activate the infinity breathing technique as well as an exercise to stimulate personal healing.

Once while working with a student enduring back pain, I asked him to begin breathing into the restricted area. I watched as his breath activated infinity lines, becoming circles of energy moving through the crystals located in the spine. The process engulfed each vertebra, creating a chain of spirals intertwining around and through the entire spinal column. As we continued to connect our breathing rhythms with this circular pattern, both of us were aware of the powerful healing in process. He experienced warmth pulsating through his whole back and felt heat concentrating in the painful area. The majority of pain was alleviated during this session.

In my continuing exploration of the infinity breath, the initial figure expanded into numerous figure eights that moved freely in all directions, activating a geometric mandala. The tingling feelings in my body were intensified and the increasing warmth of my feet indicated my deep groundedness.

When clairvoyants look at a person's field, they see what is called the Monad as the 12th chakra at a distance above the person's head approximately equal to his/her physical height. This is a fast-frequency energy center that regulates and feeds to our physical body and Soul. At one point, for me, this breathing exercise changed. My inhale began with God/Source, crossed over through my Monad and turned around at my heart—the exhale moved from my heart through my Monad to God. As I continued with this pattern my body felt ever-increasing lightness and simultaneously, a powerful feeling of connectedness to Earth.

In another experience this breathing pattern expanded into multiple infinity symbols about the Monad and the EarthCore, into an expansion beyond mental comprehension. Continuing this new breathing model, I felt my physical body begin to expand like a balloon filling with air. I felt as though I were becoming larger and larger until the whole world was inside my body. The Earth seemed to have my head, arms and legs protruding from it. The exhilaration was indescribable. Tears flowed, laughter erupted, a knowing was very present without any need to figure out or understand what was happening. The experience was so exhilarating that within days of this influx, I experienced several more intense transmissions of Spirit. To get a sense of what I felt, imagine the following:

> There is a dimension where All Is—where every being is
> able to be All at once. Here everything comes together
> then moves out and returns to One; continual movement
> in and out, up and down—the center becoming the edge,
> the horizontal becoming the vertical. In the joining and
> separating is being One.

I realized the above representations were not two-dimensional —they were multidimensional, rotating, undulating spheres.

Another time I could clearly see the center point as my Monad. There was wholeness, completeness reflected in the steps. It was as if I were being guided through each part to completely manifest the reality of the concepts. My guidance says it is imperative to remain grounded even when the spheres appear to be operating in the higher realms. I noticed the beginning figures continued in their spherical mandala—figures operating within other spheres. Later, I saw patterns from my heart into my Monad to Source, each one moving through another aspect of the 12th chakra, to another presence of myself. The heart is considered the fulcrum point between Heaven and Earth, between Father and Mother. These connect into our humanity through the Inner Male, Inner Female and Magical Child, the perfect triad of humanity and Divinity. As with most areas of consciousness, when we are willing to explore and incorporate new-to-us concepts, we first assist all parts of Self and then we assist each other.

In another meditation I was suddenly aware that these mandala figures were outside my physical body. They seemed to be present without my being part of the picture. I was very curious. Why would they operate outside my body? It was as if I were not required. *They were breathing me!* So simple, yet hidden from my consciousness until that moment. A powerful realization surfaced—every 'body' has this. It is the core of creation—regardless of form, location, or plane of existence. These figurative spheres are in every level of all fields, into infinity. And into and through every dimension, every level of existence—even beyond what we know to be. Words are too small to convey this experience.

Later I was shown how powerful it is to use this basic principle with another person, consciously creating my Soul, Heart, Earth connection; then breathing from my heart to their heart, appearing as a circle. Regardless of their mental attitudes, energetically their hearts feel recognized, loved and accepted—a valued feeling for all people.

In groups we have played with this with each person creating a mandala of infinity signs with him/herself in the center, breathing the energy from Source through her/his field into the center of the group. Love is brought forth beyond our mental comprehension. It permeates every giver, every receiver. Each participant is present in the experience without judgment, allowing Spirit to continually pour through in the capacity that is perfect for each involved—allowing, inviting, presenting. Love pours through as the healer for all.

Infinity breathing, chakra clearing and healing also are very rewarding to me. I begin with the basic connecting breaths of Soul through Heart to Earth as I open to the moment's maximum potential. It is my intention to cleanse individual chakras as I sense them one at a time. The center fulcrum might move from the Heart to individual chakras, allowing each chakra to be the center point of the figure. At other times there seems to be action in individual chakras as each is cleansed. Sometimes there have been spiralings inward and outward of what seem to be the spheres of Universes, of All That Is, of myself—everything included. For me, the spiraling frequently continues into movement through each chakra and through all 'other' lives—with envelopment, immersion, even embodiment of my planet of origin with Earth. I have sensed personal embodiment of earth, nature, pain, garbage, beauty, ugliness, life, death. Each of these identities joins the sphere that undulates in its rotation with changing colors and emerging sounds—from guttural noises to symphonies of Angelic music. All colors, all sounds, all shapes, all things, all of Creation is joined in the spirals.

    ❧ I am very grounded, using the infinity breathing with the center in my heart, letting go of where the turns are going. Quite powerful. The elongation of the figure begins to shorten, creating circles, crossing where they meet. Then on the right side of my body, they begin rolling out and down, away from me, first one circle meeting another and moving through one another, multiplying. Numerous circles connecting, within and out of one another, moving in all directions with the same rotation.

While continuing to emphasize my breath, the center moves out from my heart-chakra center to above and below. I notice nothing seems to be happening on my left side. In fact, it is difficult to pull my attention to that side. Gradually I am aware the motion is beginning there as well, except that the rotation is moving toward me. Suddenly I am in the center of all the movement—infinity into infinity.

I am floating within the motion, in the space of the circles, following the spiraling movement. Somewhere in this experience I am aware of a point of choice—and again I choose to stay in my body, on Earth. Deep breaths continue; I feel tears flowing. I keep my energy inside. My feet are very hot and seem glued to the floor—even an hour after becoming aware of my physical surroundings. Total peace, acceptance, inclusion and appreciation permeate me and I know everything is available to every one of us. It is our intention that opens these veils, bringing us into greater levels of the evolutionary process. I present blessings and gratitude for all connections. ❦

# 7 Meditation for Infinity Breathing

As SHARED in the previous chapter, this infinity breathing is a very rewarding exercise. Once this breath sequence is anchored in experience, numerous variations begin to occur. I suggest you invite your mind to watch what happens without attempting to understand whatever occurs for you. Request and be totally open to guidance from your HigherSelf. If the inhale/exhale seems to want to go another way, play with it, watching your body sensations and energy fields. Remember, there is no 'correct' way other than the way it happens for you. The key for your maximum gift in any practice is to be connected to Heart, Earth and Source.

∝

Stand, or sit if necessary, in a comfortable position with your feet, preferably bare, flat on the floor or ground. ❀

Relax your body with a couple of deep breaths. ❀

Feel your heart. ❀

Take your attention to an Earth place where you feel safe. ❀

Ask your HigherSelf to direct this process. ❀

Set your intention to connect to your Soul, however this is shown to you. ❀

With an inhale, feel your Soul energies enter into the back of your heart, between your shoulder blades. ❀

Exhale out the front of your heart, back to Soul. Do this circular Soul-to-heart-to-Soul pattern for at least six breaths. ❀ ❀ ❀ ❀ ❀ ❀

Now inhale from the front of your heart into Earth—HigherSelf will direct where in Earth your breath goes. ❀

Exhale from this Earth place into the back of your heart. Repeat this circular heart-to-Earth-to-heart inhale and exhale six times. ❀ ❀ ❀ ❀ ❀

Begin combining these circles. Using one deep breath inhale from Soul into the back of your heart, out the front of the heart into Earth. ❀ ❀

On the exhale move from Earth through the back of your heart, out the front to Soul. ❀ ❀

Inhale from Soul though your back of the heart, out the front of your heart to Earth. ❀ ❀

Continue this configuration from Soul-to-Earth and Earth-to-Soul with deep rhythmic breaths for at least two minutes. As you become comfortable with this, gradually increase the time. ❧

As you become comfortable with this conscious breathing, you will find you can do this in any position and in any place—sitting, washing dishes, while waiting at stoplights, etc. It may become so normal that you might find you are breathing this way without mental concentration. In the presence of fear, anxiety or over-stimulation, this type of breathing is a valuable tool for centering oneself, consciously connecting from Soul and Heart to Earth. When we are grounded all emotions tend to stabilize.

Consider using the following exercise to stimulate personal healing. Invite your HigherSelf to direct your experience.

While breathing in the infinity pattern, be aware of thoughts and feelings, allowing them to be or go without any interference or concentration.

Continue deep rhythmic breaths asking to be shown when to take the next step.

Be open for the positions of loops and crosses to change.

Keep breathing Soul to Heart and then directly into any place of discomfort, filling the space with Divine Light, an inherent connection between Divinity and humanity.

See the Light spiraling and cleansing the painful area.

After a few moments you will know when to open the area for the outpouring of this Light into Earth.

Fill again; cleanse and release.

Do this at least three times.

At some point the figure may become a spiraling column of Light.

Continue conscious breathing within the cleansing column.

End the healing with infinity breaths from your heart into the area of disease and down into Earth.

Use the direction of your HigherSelf.

Express your gratitude for this Divine assistance. ∝

# 8 Connection to Conscious Evolution

WALKING ON THE BEACH one morning I watched the natural rhythm of baby sand fleas in conjunction with the waves, like the movement of little coquina clams. At a certain time these almost translucent creatures dig out of the sand below the water of a receding wave to wait for the next wave. When it arrives the fleas are carried across the sand. As the water recedes they quickly bury themselves to 'do their thing' until some curious sensing stimuli bring them to the surface again to repeat the process. They are continually washed to their feeding grounds by wave action. I've watched the same sequence on outgoing tides as they move to areas where they find nourishment. The en masse recognition of just when that 'special' wave is coming is inherent in them—they just know.

This knowing is in our cells as well. Sand fleas do not attempt to stop the waves or lessen or increase the natural flow. They do not count the waves; they do not think about what they are doing. Their being in the flow of life is as natural as our breath repetitions. Unconsciously we are directed in a similar manner as we move through our lives. There comes a time when we somehow choose to be more connected to some 'director'—on a path of more cooperation with our Spirit leading us. We open to respect and honor within ourselves rather than externally demanding inclusion. It is when our ego demands to be included by others or says, "No. I want to stay in this spot," that conflict arises. Choosing to acknowledge that there may be a stimulus inherent to our species, we can surrender to the evolution of our own individualism while remaining aware of our connection to the whole of humanity.

You are complete within yourself without the requirement to be socially connected to anyone or thing in particular. As the sand fleas know just what must be done, so do you. In the evolutionary aspect you have been designed as a complex species with the power of thought and reasoning. You can look around your world and see those who seemingly let the attributes of humanity be their god. Others of you establish actions that propel you into the headwaters to ride the crest of the waves of evolution.

In this space of dedication to extending and practicing, the challenges are greater and the rewards seem more inevitable. Yet you are little aware of the magnitude of what you are accomplishing. The sand fleas can represent the circle. It takes those of you who explore to find the connecting point and begin the movement of that circle into its spiraling motion, thus finding your 'way back to God'—a senseless statement because you are God in evolutionary sequences. Each one of you. Everyone of you, including the sand fleas. Your sub-personalities, as you call them, represent those sand fleas of humanity that seem to be stuck in the circle refusing to ride the waves. As you bring awareness into your own personal human conditions, you are working with the consciousness of humanity. Your exploration of any one aspect into its depths and heights alters that condition of the whole species.

And please realize that the repercussions go beyond what

we are calling humanity. Remember the earth is only a small pebble in the scope of Creation. The ripples move into the space of All That Is, into the evolution of Creation. So be aware of what is active in your life. All of you have chosen to be forerunners.

Oh yes, there is a form of choice, made prior to this incarnation. Many of you have been playing with human incarnations for many centuries, while you have been preparing for this life. And just maybe this is only preparation for another—like the sand creatures waiting for a certain wave to ride the flow of the sea. Your present life is one of the big ones. You have choice as to how far you are willing to ride in any one lifetime. How far are you willing for Spirit to send its message through you?

This is not about ego; this is about service in a way asked for only in certain times. The sub-personalities within will have objections, encounters, withdrawal and fight, however it is progress to explore these aspects, accepting a greater understanding of possibility. Remember nothing is gospel, nothing is truth except in the moment of present awareness. You are on the edge, in the place of discovery. You feel these waves, which will take the human character and tumble it into a churning where the mind has no idea of what will come forth. We tell you, it will be a new experience, a new awareness each time—this birthing of a new *Being* of action, which will play around somewhere waiting for the next big one, the next wave of consciousness to be available.

Each person has an inherent connection to one or more specific bents of mass consciousness personality and has agreed to work with these evolutionary aspects. Consider the effect if a hundred warriors got together and, with *intention* and awareness, worked through the warrior nature to evolve its natural progression into the lover. Authors such as Robert Bly[11] and Dan Millman[12] speak of this. However, with a synthesis of consciousness, any group exploring this in a more concentrated way could quickly assist the ascension to faster frequencies. Many disciplines are dancing with various revelations about consciousness while avoiding going into the depths of their personal, individual aspects. The movement of this energy would look scary to some people and, although the leaders have the concept, they are hesitant to take it to the extremes that would crack the shell. In actuality, after centuries of warring explorations the shell is so thin it will take only a dedicated group composed of a couple of hundred people to pierce the shell. And it is this way with most personality traits, particularly those that show up so worldwide.

Control also has a thin shell. But fear is one that is now still metastasized. This one will take more energy, more people committed to exploration. So many want to remain in their places of safety, in a place of mediocrity, in a place of letting others do it for them. You who are committed to assisting in your planet's evolution find these folks all the time. Become aware of unproductive energy and accept the possibility that there is a way to move through it. Look at it as the big, bad woods or forest without an obvious path. Choose to explore it anyway. You are the captains of the ships on an unfamiliar, uncharted ocean, moving to what you have imagined to be possible. Stay your course with courage and power for the journey. God is beyond any magnitude you can imagine, as elusive as a speck of dust; more powerful than the tempest of any ocean. Be happy to fulfill your destiny to be living God-ness. ✸

A friend welcomes the process of healing with her intention to embody the lessons as she opens herself to more Light. During one session our invocation asked particular Masters and Beings of Light to assist. There was a 'past' life with a clear delineation between dark and light, where she compromised her being Light to conform with family. Her willingness to see the events through love brought understanding and clearing. As we continued she was shown another energy, tracking it between herself and someone close to her in this life, choosing to name the energy 'ugly.' When asked to look for the source of 'ugly' she was shown its connection to God. She saw that it was a twisted form of love, in this case, a plea for love from the personality.

She *asked* this expanded view of 'ugly' to penetrate into that 'past' life, into the seeming values of dark and light, to bring healing to the young girl who compromised her knowing in that time, and to any others who were open to transforming their personal connection. Her courageous and loving intentions opened a safe space for this energy to untwist, to move through its contortions and mutations, returning to its original state of Divinity. Within this transformation the energy defined as 'ugly' moved into a vibration of love beyond personality identification, expression or experience. It evolved into Divine Love with All That Is, God, Creator, Source. The connection the two of these people now have is evolving to a faster vibration, allowing old patterns and feelings to drop away.

The fields of *all who were connected* with this process received transmissions of Light, greater frequencies of Creation energy to alter their conscious awareness of judgment. Working this way within the framework that there is no time/space, she expanded this healing Light into other 'lives,' thus cleansing her whole stream. Her awareness of this new definition creates opportunities for different (re)actions from herself and others, which reflect her acceptance of these expanded energies.

The plight of hanging on to an identity from the past creates a box when we identify ourselves as this or that. A friend portrays a victim of circumstances with decisions that say she can't make lasting changes. These thoughts contribute to chronic fatigue. Because she was told she was stupid, she reads poorly and quit college after two years. Therefore she cannot get a good job. I know her as a lady with competent computer skills and wonderful insights. And she continues to attract experiences to support her healing process, including recent qualifications to complete her early childhood teaching certification.

I enjoy interaction with those who are also dedicated to self-awareness by exploring numerous avenues of guidance to develop more loving life expressions. Each of us plays our role in all interactions. Some may be warriors, seen as system-busters. They move into everything and anything with gusto as they go for the gold actively. Gatherers tend to absorb information as possibility, bridging many data streams. Dreamers connect with realms beyond Earth, exploring beyond physical reality, going on their way with no outside input. Doubters tend to say, "Prove it to me," waiting for confirmation from guides—etheric or physical —before beginning real exploration. Spectators hover on the sidelines waiting to see who does what. When something clicks in, they take it enthusiastically. Developers and adventurers bring input into focus as standard-bearers holding truth. Lovers radiate heart energy of love and compassion through whatever is presented, connected to their internal truth of tenderness and vulnerability.

There is no one way that's any better, and although each of us has a primary system, others are incorporated. In whatever situation is presented we are given opportunities to discover and stand in truth. Our dedication to personal unfolding Spirit—and Its interaction with current events—dictates which we decide to portray. Discovering our natural rhythm in relationship to our physical bodies and spiritual nature is as simple as turning over a pebble—conscious evolution includes this vehicle we live in.

 The composite energies of You as Spirit in your physical body on Earth culminate at a point about a hand's distance below your feet. Mystics have referred to this as your EarthStar, your acceptance of being physical and divine at the same time. This EarthStar is a necessary ingredient for the health of the planet. Every living aspect of Creation in physical form, whether tree, rabbit, human, sand flea or eagle, has this connection, which is held in place so long as you choose to inhabit a body. Without it, physical structures return to the complex simplicity of dirt. Expand your horizons to look at these points as trillions of pores in the lungs of the Mother, this planet you call Earth.

Through your physical vehicle you breathe the energy of Source into Its creation, Earth. As rain falls, the water moves on and through Earth, returning via these pores as steam, vapor. As you breathe you become the 'breath' of the planet, another primary connection between Source and World. Living creatures must have these two elements—water and air, Mother Father connection. All of nature contributes to this natural rhythm of giving and receiving. Consciously develop a love relationship with both elements. Recognize that as humans the intake of air is natural while you must be conscious of water intake. Nurture yourselves for the incorporation of this *Mother* energy. Dolphins and whales of your planet do the opposite; they must do something to get air. For them the more feminine aspect of being is intrinsic. For trees and plants air/water intake is a natural phenomenon.

Experience this feeling:

Be a 'pore' for the planet, breathe the purity of Source through your body into the lungs of the planet, where the 'Heart of the Mother' purifies the 'blood' of the planet—just as man's lungs interact to cleanse and feed the human body.

Your exhale returns Earth's used energies to Source to be purified, just as within your physical vehicle.

Being conscious of this can open heights and depths beyond past experiences.

Be aware that with each inhale, Source is activated, illumination is enhanced.

As breath enters the EarthStar, be aware of the circulation into the 'heart' of Earth, the crystal city where brightness explodes and debris is picked up and removed with your exhale.

*You are* breathing the Earth! ❧

The synergistic relationships of Creation are much more complex than the conglomerate human mind has explored. Be prepared to tap into information that will seem impossible, strange, incoherent, while keeping yourself open to possibilities beyond present comprehension. Note the quality of information as it is presented while letting go of any need to categorize or study the concepts. Instead, *feel* the contribution. Listen to HigherSelf direction. Watch the puzzle assemble as more pieces become available. Focus on being an instrument of evolution without needing the entire symphonic production present. Let go and ride the waves into your I Am Presence for your own adventures.

# 9 Expanded Countenance

IN EXPERIENCES or in books we are frequently asked to move into the Witness State. Just what is this? How do we know we are there? My understanding is that the Witness or Watcher is an aspect of us that is always aware of what is going on in and around us. It sees our activities as well as the Spiritual realms. It watches and knows from a space of observance, without engaging in what's happening. I refer to the space between this Witness and our mental cognizance as our awareness, another energetic aspect of us that is totally unattached—no doing, no preferences or outcomes. There is also the HigherSelf, the Soul and our Monad. One day my question was for clarity about these terms.

What is the difference between the Witness and HigherSelf? Semantics! The way you visualize it is in separation when there is no separation. So we assist your understanding. The HigherSelf knows your physical attributes—body, mind, heart, emotion, thoughts and temperament. It knows from beyond your personality traits and continually gives you signals. Separation is part of the illusory concept of life on Earth. You search outside for belonging prior to joining with the myriad parts of Your-Self. The Witness watches, is ever present and aware of everything in your field without judgment or censorship about anything. The signals are always present and become conscious when you move into an opinion-less state to let your personality/mind know God.

These faster vibrational aspects are always present, available anytime you intend connection to an expanded view of that which is active within your physical realm. One mission is to live within this awareness in all that is happening in life. You want to know the intricate workings of things; yet many are just beginning to delve into the attributes beyond how appendages work, what type of fuel is required, maintenance and so forth. Some of you know to put gasoline in your car. Others are aware of its need for oil, water and lubrication. And there are mechanics who can disassemble and repair and re-assemble. Such is with the populace's awareness of the human body. Research into the complexity of the brain, the system of body sensors, the individuation of cellular structures is ongoing. It's time to grasp the inner relationships of these parts to the whole, becoming aware of the intricacies.

The results are mirrored in Earth changes being experienced. This isn't something new. This is evolution. Do you think God has any intention of starting over? Creation continues and humans are creators. Many deplore the atomic bomb. Yes, it was an unnecessary use of technology and yet the technology had to 'be discovered.' Look at all that has been invented as a result. You are exploring another planet. Not just with your imaginations. It's happening physically. These rovers do wondrous things—directed by programs encoded by scientists. Suppose there might be a certain combination of signals that could indicate something overlooked during this programming. Your Soul would have the correct formula. And God is the aspect that created all parts. The Monad holds the overall design while Soul programs and assembles; HigherSelf directs the day-to-day program—

showing these rovers just what rock to explore. Similar to your viewing the scenes of the Mars visit from the vantage of television, the Witness watches, observes everything from a perspective of impartiality, unification and equality without needing to understand or categorize.

There are additional correlations in your individual lives. The bombs of your life can seem catastrophic—disease, divorce, death. What is experienced is a tremendous teaching, alerting you to possibilities for expressing compassion and generosity. The Witness observes all phases—re-building, re-cycling, re-arranging, exploring a new 'plan-et' of who you are. You connect to Awareness that can truly sense the super nova—Monad; you feel the rearranging, the birthing, the beauty and wonder—Soul. Each of you finds interests in this development with internal guidance from HigherSelf. The Witness watches as you explore various concepts and components, all relating to this mutual development. These aspects are passionately absorbed in your momentary activity as aliveness, appreciation and gratitude. This entelechy is God, your very make-up. You are all of these identities. Live your lives from this passion. Be the excitement of Creation. Open to the Monadic bliss, the nourishment of your Soul, the direction of your Higher-Self and Witness being your total *I Am* Presence.

This God/Monad/Soul/HigherSelf/Witness interplay is the fuel from *being* to doing. When we are driving a vehicle we have greater maneuverability in acceleration than in coasting or careening. Our attention to this moment stabilizes our energy, alerting us to divine instruction revealing our spiritual nature. When we feel totally satisfied with life and something happens outside our vision, Awareness watches and holds all that is happening without any thought or emotion. We might say it's like attention without needing anything to be other than as it is. We become Awareness as we allow ourselves to really connect to internal feelings, acknowledging their validity. We uncover a sense of ourselves as greater than the body, triggering hidden aspects of mind to begin accepting there may be something beyond its knowing. Our egos lose their stronghold as we acknowledge sensing our internal Divine Intelligence that cannot be controlled, manipulated or interrupted in Its purpose. Welcome opportunities of new input, to spur expansion and development as they enhance our physical world.

Awareness involves taking the mind into the space of Oneness, into truth, moving through and beyond the antics of ego. It is the ego that perpetuates separateness as spaces of immense disconcordance between the many aspects of your human selves and God-Selves. For in truth there is no difference, yet you learn this seeming difference so well it is difficult to reunite the parts. Begin to accept the possibility of *everything being God*— every movement, every event, every thought and emotion—all that you see, feel, hear, smell, or taste. Every feeling is communication from Soul to our Awareness, encouraging exploration into any resistance to having God as every thing in your reality.

Consciousness includes all that you are aware of. Subconscious is conditioning that runs your life. You don't know what is there and yet it shows up in behavior, business ethics and social conduct, attempting to confuse personal truth expressions. You have been taught that it is inadvisable to let unknown parts express. When patterns and their related emotions come up, you cut them off without cognizant expression. Instead they show up in dreams, nightmares, fantasy and fascination. Shoving things back in the corner is a lack of acceptance.

Personality is the distinctive quality or character of being a particular person, the manner of action. It develops according to the genetic composition of the chromosomal structures at conception. As the energies of other people are presented, your thoughts/beliefs about these realities form the ego. This keeper of your external reality is used by the mind to control behavior. Mind defines, categorizes, judges and worries, runs your lives, using your past to program the future, totally ignoring the present. It is the base of problems, the basis of fear, while saying it can do everything from its illusionary place of power. Both personality and ego tell the mind what is real. You project out of this context until the discovery of YourSelf encourages this deeper knowing to surface.

All are useful; do not think you will rid yourselves of these valuable aspects. The personality is the gatekeeper, the one who screens comings and goings. You learn to alter its directives or its job description by changing its rules about who/what enters the gate. Every time a part of the personality has a growth adventure and successfully proceeds into the next rank of Spirit, energy changes noticeably.

Consider personality as the energy between lessons to learn and daily experience—always a two-way street of the emotional/mental body's interrelationship with Essence and physicality. The twisting and/or constriction of alignment interacts with ego, playing out the restriction until you decide you've had enough. This decision relaxes the emotional/mental restrictions, opening for Spiritual energies to work in and through these bodies. If distortions occur in the mental or emotional bodies, Spiritual energies are rerouted or detoured and sometimes blocked. When the obstruction becomes too great the molecules become undernourished spiritually and physicality is interrupted—disease begins. Spaces shrink so the undernourished molecules begin to stick to one another. The 'threads' from the etheric body become twisted, adhering to one another. There is no healthy sequence to these 'stickies'; they become a jumbled mass. The etheric body, your physical blueprint, is altered and the clear energetic current is restricted, creating dysfunction at the cellular level, which interferes with the natural flow of Essence. Frequently the threads appear as large, dense rope. As you remove the layers you are disentangling the fibers into very fine structures—cleansing. Spirit once again flows freely into all aspects of your cells.

God and the personality/mind/ego are one—the personality is the thought; God is the gap between thoughts. This expanded awareness supports the merging of ego into the Trinity of I—ego, personality and mind. Self is this trinity that connects to Source Oneness through HigherSelf and Soul. It has no form, no conceptualization or understanding, no separate parts as it is the trinity of everything together. It is also part of another trinity formed at birth—Earth, as physical matter, the incarnation of Soul as Self, and Spirit/God/Source.

When we *be*, there is a natural flow into activity that is directed from that deep heart space that knows all outcomes, knows the perfection. All aspects of us, physical and spiritual, are in holographic relationship for this opportunity for life to love life. This activates the spiral of Creation that dictates when, what and where the optimum experience is for each of us. Miracles happen as we recognize we are our own heroes, opening to the unexpected without any ideas or motivation. God is beyond any magnitude we can imagine. Our lives are our reality of God presenting Itself.

*Flow, Spirit, flow, and all my fears release,*
*I am a channel for Thy love and peace.*
*Fill me with power and let my heart be strong.*
*Fill me with joy that I may sing Thy song.*
*Heal, Spirit, heal, and all my self renew.*
*I am expressing my perfection true.*
*Fill me with love that I may loving be.*
*Fill me with life that I may live for Thee.*

Maori Folk Melody[13]

# 10  Expanding Time

WE KNOW we can be aware of many things going on around us while we are doing in the moment and yet physically we are only where we are doing what we are doing. The washing machine is running while dinner cooks in the oven as mother prepares a salad while dessert is cooling in the fridge as she listens to the children's laughter with gratitude that this particular TV station's programming supports children. She checks the clock wondering if hubby will arrive on time, remembering that last week he was late so the girls had to wait for her before beginning the bridge game. She really dislikes arriving after everyone is there since her clothes are not from the latest designer knowing she is waiting to loose those extra pounds before going on another shopping expedition which reminds her of the whipped cream to go on the dessert and that she will have only a very small serving since Suzie always has such luscious creations to share on their game nights.

Meanwhile father is driving home with intentions of letting go of his day at the office while reviewing the board meeting bringing thoughts about all the details of this project that must be completed by Friday. He must ask Hank to be really careful filling out those forms to be presented to the director day after next. It is imperative that the wording be such as to prevent any other interpretation of the overall objective. He is aware that this is his evening with the children as it's Eve's night to play bridge and wonders if there will be any time for him to go over this one report a little deeper, remembering Danny needs extra help with his algebra. Quickly his attention is brought to the road and traffic as someone weaves his car in and out of the multiple lanes in what he thinks is an unsafe manner, while his peripheral vision notes children playing with a huge dog in a field, triggering memories of the way Rover loved to catch a Frisbee until his master left home for college.

Our internal conversations traverse all aspects of the past to re-present the present. Living *Now* is a vulnerable place, opening oneself to everything, every aspect of Creation.

Interrupt patterns by verbalizing wants and desires in the moment without concentrating on what is happening around you. Become conscious of your awareness by talking to yourself. Say what is true right now. And right now. Begin in your personal time. Speak out loud—every thought, feeling, emotion. You will begin to notice repeated patterns that surface from past experiences rather than the present situation. You may feel that while you are speaking there is another part of you noticing something else. Enhancing your awareness of this Self integrates your multiplicity into Oneness.

As I have played with verbalization in the moment I've developed a greater sense of mind, personality and ego connection. I began noticing a difference in any expressions. Mind was adamant, personality connected with wants and desires, while ego contradicted. Gradually it was as if they realized all three couldn't express at once and they finally blended together. At first this alignment continued to pull me out of the moment, however as I continued speaking thoughts out loud to myself, I realized a feeling of incorporation where past and future melded into right now. A presence of peace expanded. I see this as a shot through the constraints of time into unbounded freedom.

❧

Explore with this adventure into *Now:*

Begin your adventure by verbally describing how your body feels, all sensations as you become aware of them.

Describe any ideas about doing this exercise—including criticism or judgments.

Avoid wondering why.

In this exercise the mind may start tagging memories onto the present, recalling some experience or story.

Stay out of the past; be aware and listen to *Now.*

Breakthrough happens *Now*—not then, not when.

Say what is *Now*—one word, then two words, maybe three. Keep it short. Sentences are too much.

Be totally aware of your body and your feelings.

Use absolute honesty in every moment.

Speak your inner voices.

Be in truth about the present to experience a totally new space, a 'stretch' where time really stops.

Experience speaking in this manner with another person who agrees to support you.

When one is in truth this way, one lives without the restrictions of time.

Time stands still ❧

At times it's as if we run up against ripples in our life experience. Some sap our energy—similar to climbing a steep hill—while others are almost unnoticed except that something out of the ordinary happens. I am shown these ripples as energy tucking back on itself, where something was incomplete in former interactions, some experience was left with ends dangling. Another opportunity to be with this person for fresh interchanges from today's perspectives. Another chance to acknowledge our energy, to create balance. Many times no physical person is involved with me since it could be energy left over from another lifetime. It is my perceptions that create my waves. The other person(s) might never experience any ripple. Balancing these relationships with present reality smoothes out the wrinkles.

During hypnotherapy training I was fascinated by explorations into other lives, going into another 'time.' I delved into numerous biographies investigating some titillating scenes—never discovering any rich and famous characters. The powerful avenue in these experiences is discovering the ripples that interfere today with loving respect for every interaction. One day I was directed to re-create activities and interpretations of 'my' character (never that of another), thus changing a past time frame. I wondered if I were making it up, however more than a year later in a subsequent visit to that lifetime, the scenes were like ancient photographs. Although the original scenes were there I was surprised to discover my activities had changed. I was not participating where I used to be, but in the ongoing recreated scenes. Present-day relationships with associated people changed in today's experiences. I had a new perspective about our interactions. Clients have also experienced alterations in their energy stream with corresponding changes in their relationships to particular people.

Most of us have had unexplainable emotional reactions with certain activities, people, locations, smells and so forth. As we are aware we can ask our HigherSelf to assist in an investigation to broaden our understanding. A very memorable one for me was while visiting the museum established by the Makah Indians in Neah Bay, Washington. Housed there are artifacts uncovered from the coastal community of Indians who lived in Ozette about 500 years ago. A gigantic mudslide had entombed the inhabitants during their sleep. The discovery has captivated the interest of archeologists because it's one of the rare instances where neither fire nor warfare had ravaged an excavated village. I had such curiosity about the details of excavations, exhibits and present preservation methods. It was as if I approved of what was being done. I asked myself why.

In the long house, I sat in silence for more than twenty minutes. Emotions ranged from love to anger. I felt other energies present with me. I saw myself as a healthy young male standing under a shoreside thatch-roofed structure, sand under my feet. (In this peninsula area the coast is composed of smooth, black stones.) I was smoothing a long board with a large piece of shell. Another interesting aspect was that I had on no clothes, not even a loincloth.

Later as I continued through the exhibition I wondered about what I had 'seen.' The background behind one exhibit showed sandy beaches! At the end of the tour was a gift shop where one of the pen and ink sketches of village activities portrayed a man standing on large rocks with spear ready for some sea creature. He was naked! I asked the shopkeeper about the pictures. Yes, the beach was sand in that time and place. He explained that clothing was a scarcity and worn only for travel or ceremony. For me, this validated my being part of that community, thus the intense emotional response as I walked through the exhibit.

Another powerful experience was in Hot Springs, South Dakota, in the museum that houses a large excavation of mammoth remains. This day there was no digging. By the time I had gone about two-thirds around the hole, tears were surfacing. I felt a strange mixture of sadness and elation. I *knew* something, some truth that was presently beyond my comprehension. Strange that in this place there were no signs of human habitation. I left the building for fresh air, concentrating on grounding my energy, and then returned to take a slower tour of the site. Similar emotions underscored some unknown ancient connection to this scene.

Clarity came later while riding down the road. I 'saw' the lush plains, the magnificent animals and vegetation, Garden of Eden qualities of balanced habitation. My whole body shook. Symphonies of sound and colors exploded, almost making me breathless. I could visualize us as non-physical visitors to this paradise, the materialization of ecstatic tones and hues. There are no words to describe the rapturous, sensual beauty. It was our vacation land, a place of rest and relaxation. No human artifacts were present because none were needed—we created out of the diverse energies present without need to leave anything behind. Everything was available. And then we decided to have another experience of Creation.

How did these adventures change my life? In addition to expanding my consciousness, they opened vistas to explore beyond the confines of time to possibilities about other realities and to release many perceptual judgments. Living and accepting these experiences prepared me to accept other perplexing theories, particularly about our representation of time—offering numerous "What if..." considerations.

Aliveness is not knowing, living the question in the moment, being in our center including everything. Excitement, joy, meditation, inner dialogue, chores, work and play are all aspects of life wherever and whoever we are. Be present in all Presence—the gift of peaceful awareness within every *Being* for this earth plane. Maybe time is to be spent eating a cookie, gazing at a flower, searching in a stream or rolling down a hill.

Intimately *be* the moment—the only time Creation exists. Is there a way to remember and be present without being caught in time? Maybe this is the game, the experiment. Let's live.

# 11 The Flow of Creation

Sometimes it takes seeing the simplicity of possibilities in order for the mind to grasp the complexity of the whole. Like eating a mountain one bite at a time. See a sphere that is complete, totally fulfilled within itself, having explored every aspect of itself. Now see another. They have their similarities and yet within their makeup is the freedom of their individual completeness—their genetic code. Without one another their wholeness is all they can be. The act of coming together brings forth aspects for either to experience beyond their existence. Something outside one form is necessary for development beyond the original.

When the sperm and egg unite, each element has the other's individuality to explore, a unique combination of each original sphere—their similarities and differences. Creation is an experiential cluster of spheres with each cell having its inherent qualities *and* being part of the whole.

Visualize your lives as a replica of this concept. You are the combination of sperm and egg—immediate conception of physical formation. Your personality follows this model, developing with every experience you encounter from the moment of conception. Another cluster touches you; there is a common expression. You come together, you experience, you integrate. Every one is a sovereign expression of the original, complete within itself; however, evolution requires interaction to fuel further development. With each encounter, every cluster of spheres is uniquely impacted in relationship to its inherent code.

Each of you has experienced times when you resisted something that seemed fun. Even if you were aware of the possibilities, you refused to cooperate because it would take you into another location or you would have to leave or give up something. The energy becomes as the balloon squeezed in the middle, restricted into past and/or future with little movement in the present. This is very disruptive in your spiral of life and yet, because it is your decision, Soul must go along with your choice. However, at some time in your life, this next experience will surface again. Each successive time there will be more urgency creating less choice on your part as to whether to participate willingly. Consider the times when you seemed forced into some avenue you would not choose where the consequences were very upsetting. These may represent conglomerations of past refusals. While, also represented, may be an experience of shock or chaos or the greatest love you recall ever experiencing. All expressions of humanity are experienced in one lifetime or another. When something is left undone, some future aspect of you returns to take care of it. Energetically it is much easier to clean everything in the process of each moment.

Feelings are to be honored without being discounted by automatic responses. The words we connect to feelings denote their significance in our lives according to past experiences. Like feeling good, getting angry, upset or hurt is an emotional choice. Something happens and anger surfaces. Mind jumps in saying anger is bad. And yet we are feeling the experience, feeling in motion—e-motion. If our definition of the feeling has been previously judged as bad, we berate ourselves for being in that emotion, frequently denying it—like burying the toilet under the living room rug.

Regardless of what message from the past mind is giving us, being present with our feelings is one aspect of the process called awakening. We integrate mind rather than having mind use us. Love and joy and understanding emerge as we embody compassion for our humanness. We live in choice—until we discover a freedom beyond choosing, the place of "Thy will be done."

Let's remember that *this* moment is our greatest opportunity. What happened yesterday is gone; tomorrow is still out there. Being conscious of *now*, no matter what the feelings, instigates a greater opening for God's Love to pour in and through us. We are served by being very present with what is happening, holding the highest Spiritual intent for all interactions and ourselves. Spontaneity is vulnerability, risking and being excited about life. We are not inadequate. There is no lack. Aliveness is an inherent aspect of living the questions and responding to the opportunities of every moment. Create consciously. Be holographic Divine potential in action.

# 12 Perfection

Sometimes we are drawn into thought patterns that tell us everything that matters is outside this moment, that we have to do this or that to *reach* some attainment existing only in the future or another life beyond present conditions and place. When we connect to the attributes of right *now* we discover there are measures of security, comfort, support and happiness heretofore hidden from our view. Discovering self-empowerment and letting life live us keeps us in *Now*, following its momentum. Saying "yes" to this flow gives such flexibility, instigating accessible rhythm. If we choose to 'think about' it, the opportunity moves on, the window closes. Here or there, always another perfect experience, another perfect opportunity of life. Within our own Self is fulfillment and joy in the condition referred to as 'Heaven within.'

For years, with little connection to what it means, I heard about perfection and the possibility that everything is perfect just as it is. I wondered how there could be perfection when there was so much unhappiness, disaster, and illness. My investigation uncovered more questions than answers. As I continued to hold the questions, examples of possibility were revealed. I saw how if this and this were not happening I wouldn't have the opportunity for this particular interaction. Had I not been Sue's friend, her Aunt Mag would have been left out of my life. Could this be some of what *perfection in the moment* was referring to? I've heard of Buddha's expression of everything being perfect—there is nothing to share or teach, nothing to change. Sharing with another or another sharing with me in whatever modality is perfection of the moment. None of the participants could have received or given this particular event at any other time. We weren't ready. The puzzle pieces were not aligned. This moment amplifies revelations of prior moments with consummate unfolding perfection.

This understanding of perfection of the moment has opened up numerous doorways for growth for me. Through directions I received to let go of all attachment to definition and identification I overcame one big hurdle. At that time I was asked to look deeper—especially into the energies held by my life's emotional positions. I saw how wants, desires and dreams are attachments that take us out of the moment. They create obstacles that clog our life flow. Wanting something to be other than the way it is or to make something happen or change reflects doubt in perfection—creates space for ego control. That place beyond wants is life in the continual 'go' lane, the green light of vitality. Ram Dass[14] suggests the only reason to be in life is to be free. Freedom is void of personal attachment. We can honor all aspects of self *just as they are*—habits, views, health, neurosis, relationships, job. As we look at what is present, noting particularly where constriction shows up, we open our inherent ability to change perceptions beyond the seeming necessity to believe or act in any certain way. We remove the obstacles that have obstructed the view of our connection to God.

Judgments are beliefs that are outdated and ready for transformation, portrayed as confusion, anger, suspicion, betrayal and other qualities related to a lack of our trusting ourself. Trust is an aspect of love, for without love, one does not trust. Judgment jumps right in there to say some unrecognized part is actively evaluating ourselves, transferring our energy externally. When we become aware of judgment, we can question and examine that moment to find clues about what these energies represent. It's like dropping a rock in a pot of vegetable soup. The soup surrounds and encompasses the foreign object. No judgment that a rock doesn't belong in vegetable soup. Ego dominates, sees the rock as something foreign, not 'right,' producing various thoughts to justify its stance. Spirit sees the whole and all the parts as the Is-ness of soup.

The act of defining anything contributes to its presence and supports its growth, frequently into a space of greater distress. In accepting the perfection of the moment without judgment, we support the emergence of a new paradigm of experience—doing from the space of *being*, where actions are clean and prosperous. It is when we are attached *to any* outcome that we step out of the stream, losing the flow of highest manifestation. It's an act of God Love that enables us to experience this reflection of *being* out of harmony with Divine Truth. True unfoldment cannot be directed or programmed; it is always disconnected from illusory distortions. Its natural flow erupts from the internal Essence of Love and compassion to support the evolution of Soul experiences.

Make way for every experience, every thing—pure Essence of God. Our birthright is harmonious reawakening to our Spiritual heritage, which is always present within us. Others can mirror the principles, but it is up to each of us to uncover all the embellished rationalizations we use to deny our Essence qualities.

ﾟﾟ Incidents of personality's idea of unfairness kaleidoscope across my consciousness one after another as feelings wind down, down, down into contraction— until I burst into hilarious laughter. My body rocks and then begins to spiral uncontrollably. (There is a part of me that knows I can stop this 'nonsense' at any time and doesn't understand why I continue.) I hold my abdomen in its laughter-associated spasms while tears of sadness begin to flow. Feelings of what might have been wash through my body. Screams erupt; then my body begins to relax as I accept what was as all that could have been. Noticing the shallowness of my breath, I concentrate on deep breaths that come into my heart and out through all the pores of my body, producing relaxation. I hear the message, "All is well" and begin infinity breathing until calming peacefulness fills me in swirling colors. I am lying on the floor, arms and legs askew.

[Such incidents show parts of me holding unproductive memories. I can choose to flow with the energies into healing whatever inconsistencies I am shown, or I can choose to ignore them. My preference is to feel the energies for the emergence of new perceptions.]

✒ After a short silence I slip into integration and mediation. Out of darkness of 'night sky' comes a silver comet into my field. The stars twinkle. Then the voices.

We are the sparkles from beyond exploration. We are ones to support you. We come from/with Love to assist you, connect with you in Love. We are your Spiritual Family. Continue your work. We support you in every venture. Be open. Be willing. We are with you. There is much more information coming. Have trust, patience. Stay open. Now you are feeling us. Continue. The pain around your head was our signal; now we can change this. Thanks for your recognition.

✒ Emotions well from my depths; tears of gratitude begin. The feeling of loving acceptance is powerful. I stay in the feeling. All lights send their 'comet' to me. I am totally surrounded. The feeling continues. Then I am 'out there,' watching me here. The background turns green, flooding my body. I feel lifted, exhilarated, totally present with All That Is. Everything and nothing meld into One. Tones of Angelic music manifest. I hear an aria of beauty that moves into critical mass, flows through nature, through any and all particles of energy—from the most minute to the largest collection. I see colors undulating, flashing, mixing and expanding. I view the entire scope of frequencies. Color and sound surround me, engulf me in the orchestration of Unification. I become aware of an undulation of my body, a very minute physical movement in the beginning. As I acknowledge the feelings the undulations become more active, yet the physical movement is minuscule compared to the gyrations and dancing of the colors and tones I feel. I welcome all of this experience into my total Being. ✺

Two-dimensionally your energy fields seem stationary—illusionary reality. You talk of them vibrating; it is actually an undulation, a continuous movement in space. It is a dance, a flowing movement. When you are feeling these connections in your reality, you are becoming the movements of these fields. Your physical body is being incorporated *into* your energy field, encompassed as a physical feeling for you. Your awareness of this embraces all of your *Beingness*, therefore encompassing All That Is. Although it has always been exactly as it is, you are becoming aware of the immensity of this energy in a tangible way. It seems as if you are floating in the sea—a sea so protective that regardless of how extreme the movement of the 'waters' becomes, you are floating and undulating within the sea of All That Is. It is a space of complete trust in who you are, of the *I Am Presence* that moves through re-creation.

This Promised Land can only be found within your experiencing the evolution of God manifesting All That Is. Your connecting to outside fulfillment is false assurance of fulfilled love, the pain of searching for the God you *know* exists. The secret is where you look. Grandiose concepts have hidden the truth—that God is everything, *even the pain*. Use pain and challenge as windows to another view of God's nature—so expansive as to let you do exactly as you want without interference.

❦

Play with this exercise:

Be in a place of receptivity to your Soul connection and feel these statements.

"I am God."

Sit with this a few moments noticing what happens in your body and mind.

Now use this statement: "God is me."

Is there a difference in your responses?

Where do you feel each to be more active?

In the mental body?

The emotional body?

Is there any connection between the two?

Are you more connected to one statement than the other?

There is no 'right' way, only an opportunity to know yourself differently.

There is no separation in anything you see, touch, feel, or sense—the space of complete unification.

Accept that you *can* feel this. It is always in you. You never leave this. It has been, is always happening.

Feel your heart area.

Feel the movement up into the thymus gland. Move with the energy.

Allow the feelings to express.

Incorporate all that is occurring while knowing everything is perfect.

Practice being here, and when you realize you have 'forgotten,' open yourself to return your consciousness to the connection of this experience. ❧

Physicality cannot be without these energies of inherent aliveness. It is the Creation process. Everything created is ItsSelf in perfect combination—not just physical attributes but the complete interpretation of God that you represent. You accept this when you see a field of flowers, each portraying its uniqueness. You look at an expanse of rocks and accept their differences. Why this determination to do things the way someone else does? Why any stigma of being different, of wanting different things, of doing it another way? Each individual is the entelechy of Creation. You are your Soul on a journey to be lord and master of your individual life, to embody the deep Love of God in every aspect of your Self. To do this, you have need of you, them, of every representation in your life. Acknowledge every aspect of Self, negative and positive, being aware of all that is present with and without reinforcing it.

Use your idea of love to discover new ways of expressing the perfection of your divine imagination, thus learning other ways to *Be* love. Happiness is *Being aware* at the level of present consciousness. Lower vibrational levels feel uncomfortable because they perpetuate contraction. Higher ones feel expansive—stimulating pleasurable physical responses. When your consciousness is focused in present vibrations, this pleasure expresses into the emotion of joy, stimulating happiness that responds with passion. Flow with your life, with self-nurturing and appreciation. Live passion; connect to the bliss of aliveness, continually expressing gratitude for your unique expression of perfection in its relationship to all things. ❊

We are the source for *everything* in our lives. The perfection of this moment is the motion of our response to life. If we *could* stand still, every thing, every thought would pass us by as does the stream around the rock in its midst. And even there, the rock is subjected to the elements of the changing water flow. Constant coming in and going out—change, death, birth, change. Possibly the primary purpose of Life is to move deeper into God.

| | |
|---|---|
| *Love is feeling God's perfection* | *Love is God feeling perfection* |
| *Peace is being God's perfection* | *Peace is God being perfection* |
| *Joy is expressing God's perfection* | *Joy is God expressing perfection* |

# 13  Meditation into the Essence of Spirit

WITH GROUPS AND INDIVIDUALS I have used this breath meditation to initiate an expanded consciousness of personal Spiritual connection. It opens a clearer channel to receive the Essence of Spirit. Center yourself and relax as you slowly read and experience this energy influx.

∾

The Essence of Spirit, the Essence of God rides on the breath. Breathe in this Essence—as much as you choose. ❀

Invite it to spread throughout your body. ❀ ❀

When you feel the body is full, invite this energy to fill all the fields around the body. ❀ ❀

Invite this Essence to move through you into Earth.

You may want to imagine your feet in the mud, in a river bottom; or feel the grass, hug a tree. Use whatever symbols facilitate your giving to Earth. ❀

Consider the possibility that Earth *is* filled with love. ❀

Continue to breathe in Essence. ❀

Whatever sensations are happening in the body, just let them be. They are Divine Perfection. ◉

Acknowledge the power of God, ◉

of Divine Love, ◉

of All That Is. ◉◉

Realize there is nothing for you to do. It is a matter of setting your intention for conscious connection and watching the body breathe. ◉◉

Rest in this energy, however it feels. ◉◉

You will come into a space of stillness, into nothingness. It happens. ◉◉

You are the expression of God no matter what you do. ◉◉

Be aware of all you are feeling, sensing, continuing the invitation to the Essence of God as it penetrates your Being. ◉◉◉

Breathe deeply and steadily as you continue to receive and give this Essence. ◉◉

Notice the feelings in your heart area. ◉◉

Whatever thoughts pop into mind, welcome them as part of right now—this divine moment. ◉◉

Become aware of your whole physical body. ◉◉

Breathe into any place where restriction is felt. ◉

When you are ready, slowly notice the seat that is supporting you. ◉

You feel safe and refreshed.

Take two deep breaths to bring your awareness to your physical location. ❋

Be aware of whatever perceptions are present. ❋

You can set the intention to hold these feelings, this space of quietness, as long as you choose. ᑉ

# 14  Access Spirit's Knowing

"Who are you?" said the Caterpillar.

Alice replied rather shyly, "I – I hardly know, Sir, just at present—at least I know who I was when I got up this morning, but I think I must have been changed several times since then."[15]

ONE DAY a friend wanted me to ask my guides a particular question. When I tuned in they were laughing, rolling with laughter. "Such a trivial concern. There is no answer," they said. "If only you humans would lighten up and stop worrying, picking at things. Just let them go." It was funny. We both joined their laughter and felt very light.

Do we ask questions to make us delve deeper into ourselves or to really receive answers? Our desire to know is triggered by unconscious attempts to understand our real heritage. "How are you?" seems like a greeting of interest and yet most of us are aware of instances where the solicitor had no interest in really knowing anything about us. Sometimes asking such a question acts as an invitation for the respondee to relate long stories about his or her reality. Being aware of conditions while noting associated feelings brings sensitivity to the situation. Asking with awareness of specific motives is more supportive of the questioner and the respondent.

With continued interaction there are times when questions can assist the speaker to focus, particularly one who is unaccustomed to really sharing depths of self. Carefully worded questions serve to instigate delving into what is really happening rather than acknowledging the surface layer where the mind is comfortable. Such questions as "How do you feel about that?" send a signal of true interest with sensitivity and kindness without expectations about what will be said or done. Whereas, "What are you feeling?" engages the mind to speak about the situation rather than taking the attention into the body for the authentic answer.

Regard each question as a stimulus for contemplation to lead into expanding awareness. We frequently ask someone outside ourselves when we seek to become aware of our internal objective. Yet conscious inward questioning spurs inner contemplation that leads to new awareness. I find when questions pop up about present conditions in my life and I consciously ask myself for the answer, I usually receive very clear answers. When the inquiry relates to other people, answers are often revealed in their activities or conversation, thus eliminating my need to ask. If this fails to occur, the question and answer relates to a mind game and is of no real importance in my life. There are so many things I don't need to know. Being too curious about details can drain personal energy. William Elliott quotes Ram Dass as saying, "The whole world will become an answer to our question. Everything in my life is an answer to my question."[16]

Part of your nature is that for nine months your developing physical body pushes the womb, your multiplying cells program growth, then physically you complete this cycle by being born. However, energetically it continues. Look at your propensity for 'a little more,' a little farther, a little faster—dessert, money, drink, status.

This occurs within energetic fields as well. You explore a concept, ask a question. There is always an answer and at times valuable ones come from outside sources. However the most potent answers are from the internal questioning that pushes your envelope to expand knowledge, expression and experience. Your content is enhanced—new possibilities, new realms of understanding. Those of you who push the envelope move actively along the path of evolution, examining exploration possibilities and cultivating your curiosity of what is beyond present conditions. Here you find answers to questions you didn't even ask. This pushing the envelope is different than your term 'pushing the water.' The envelope is an energetic representation of your next growth plane and when you attempt to push the water you are working in counteraction to the natural flow of your life.

An important aspect of asking is listening—listening internally for that inner voice. Being caught up in the peculiarities of what is happening outside your realm produces static resonance in your field. You are stimulated by numerous outside influences that the mind hangs onto as if they were reality. Detach from details that are out of context with the present moment. Until you have personally experienced the creative energy of any concept, it is just junk hanging out in your field. Let go of needing to know, of needing to understand. Go with personal experience and feel your potential expand.

When you are open to internal Spirit messages, clarity comes from everyday events. There is no need to be in a particular place or mood, in meditation or asking specific questions. Answers come through your attention to momentary stimuli in daily interactions—conversations, headlines, books, music, and movies.

We have previously shown you how the energies of want, desire, dream, etc. take the lazy route into manifestation and the advantage of using intention as the fastest stream to connect to creation.[17] Now we speak about 'ask.' Asking goes way beyond childhood experiences when requests were made. As one moves into the state of *Beingness* one uses intention to create, which comes through the conceptions of your imagination into creation. What occurs is not a passive energy; there are magnificent explosions of energy that accompany any creation. It is like an inventor perceiving an idea, visualizing how it could look and then creating form— whether it be an object or a corporation. When the process moves from the state of intentional conception into the actual creation, the inventor must do something—ask for materialization. This transference from *Being* into doing stimulates conception to form.

The action of asking creates an opening, allows forces that have congregated around the intention to materialize; otherwise they are still supporting the intention. When you have an intention that is strictly personal in nature, that does not need assistance from others, a degree of manifestation can occur. However, when asking is included, the stream of joint forces is opened to fully manifest the intention. Using meditation and prayer to communicate personal views, feelings and images brings assistance from other realms. For the optimum results, all of this is accompanied with a deep heart connection. Watch the actions of children; they know how to ask. A child asks over and over, for he knows the world is to support his every need, until he receives or until reactions around him are less than positive.

What happens to the adult who is the recipient of the asking? If they are in accord with the request they gladly respond with positive results. About the fourth or fifth time they hear a request, their energy frequently moves into their power center to activate control to stifle the requester. Or they move into judgment wondering how anyone could be so stupid, so persistent. "Leave me alone. Can't you see I'm busy?" "No, that isn't good for you." "Go find something better to do."

There are experiences to do alone, ways to experiment and methods to employ. All it takes is love. In the end you all have to do *it* yourself. Ask for intercessory assistance. Ask for a hug, for someone to play with. Honor your own expressions.

Here is a refinement of manifestation energy to consider. As you live from the faster frequencies of love you become ready to expand your energy from mental 'intention' into connecting to the divine aspect of Self through heart space. Ask, "What is required to bring forth my intention." And then listen. This may be with physical people, from within your personal energy stream, or with Guides, Angels, Masters. Just remember to ask from the connected space of your *Being* to create the opening for total manifestation. And let go of all attachment to any outcome—now or later. Focus on what is present, continuing to ignite your Presence of Divinity while listening for any steps you can take to facilitate the process. Be willing to be used. Be appreciative of all assistance without attachment to how, when or where. *Be Present!*

One April I followed an intention—that of attending a seminar held yearly in Bali by a leader I'd met in 1992.[18] I knew that someday I would make this journey. My attempts to get a ticket were futile, no available seats at the right time. I asked for direction and let go. Weeks later during meditation I heard the word Bali. One telephone call confirmed airline tickets had opened for the right time and price. The next month, away I went—eighteen hours by plane, flying through two days.

Easter morning I sat in this plane over some part of the Pacific Ocean after twelve hours of flying in darkness. My experience of the sunrise was exhilarating. All colors were present. Reds to orange to yellow to green and blue into the indigo of the still dark western sky, pinpointed by stars sprinkled in the crown of Creation. The perfection in the blending colors—the reds moving into yellow creating orange, the yellow moving into the blue creating greens, turquoise, the blue into its darker value that reflects the reds again to create the indigo purple. The rainbow for sunrise! The spiral of color, the perfection of Creation called the dawn—a place where each of us creates through our own perceptions. Joy. Joy. Joy and immense gratitude ran through my system echoing divine energy spiraling through my body. The beauty in existence, in life, in love, in flow, in *being* human. The realization, the creation of our I Am reality. We are risen when we claim our Divinity, our connection. We can raise our consciousness, our connectedness, our awareness of God in action through our lives.

Experiences expand past mental records that have directed how we do, feel and think. Judgments and attitudes of certainties and absolutes frequently warp these recollections. Answers present numerous possible actions, like taking sand out of a barrel grain by grain. The ego resists consistent repetition, wanting something it sees as more rewarding. Meditating with breath, mantras or chants are avenues beyond ego and personality intervention. Being open to the unexpected allows every question, interaction, feeling and thought to be noticed and loved. By the time we come to a feeling of completion that we call insight, original questions are absent while others take their place. Insights arise from seemingly unanswerable questions triggering us into deeper revelations of Divine Wisdom. Every moment is an opportunity to be present with what is happening right now, enhancing awareness of how we act and react.

❧

Play with this exercise:

You are in the activities of today. A good friend, your spouse or your children say, "Let's go swimming."

What is the first thought that arises—before anything else?

Is it for or against this activity?

Is there a voice that says, "Yeah, that would be fun."?

Or does it present reason after reason why going swimming would not be a good thing?

How long does it take you to move into consideration of the idea *from this moment* rather than automatically responding from past experiences or reacting with projections about all the things that need to be done?

Mind's agenda automatically programs your lives against any suggestion that takes immediate action—it always evaluates how your safety or survival is involved.

As you learn to be present accepting that your heart knows this moment and knows what love can do, you begin to follow your heart for life to be rich and full. ❧


One such blessing occurred on a Spring day while I was in Saint Augustine, Florida, for a workshop. My coordinator and I were walking on the beach when we spotted a baby warbler that had flown too close to the water and was being washed by the tide. It allowed me to pick it up. We talked of how natural it felt to walk along cradling this aspect of nature. As if we were the ones to make such decisions, we discussed what to do with it. Forty minutes later we were approaching the car when a gust of wind assisted the bird in its flight from my hand to my shoulder, then to a beach chair and into the grass by a cottage. The breeze had dried its feathers. We experienced its trust, the wonder, beauty and sharing. It presented an opening for each of us, looking into how and when we are open to trust so unquestionably that we can be held when we need be. Blessed were we by the experience, by this mirror of nature reminding us to stay present in the precious moments. *Being* brings unusual events to enhance our lives moment to moment.

In any interaction there are diverse aspects that feel 'right.' As the grocer, the baker, the candlestick maker, we support one another along the way by creating focus to assist, stabilizing expansion. We question ourselves; we ask others, and there are still questions. For me Masters and Angels are way-showers, assistants of the direct path, impressing us with ideas, ways of being with Love. It is up to us to receive.

Empowered way-showers, whether physical or etheric, have no energy invested in what we do, no requirements for us to be or do certain things. Their energy is invested in being of service, of assisting our requests. They are benevolent, complete within themselves with no attachment to any outcome. They embody a deep sense of caring and compassion. Each of them demonstrates its sovereignty, its love for humanity, and they take care of themselves. Let us teach ourselves and welcome guidance from these loving *Beings* as they invite us to open our hearts to the embodiment of our Essence connection to our own state of sovereignty.

To open your field even more, use *allow*. Feel this energy; experience the expansion this creates. Invite your choice to come into this opening. *Intend* the action you are willing to be part of. And ASK for assistance. Just as you *allow* someone to enter your home by opening the door, you invite this person in with *intention* and *ask* for his or her service. Consider these identities:

A – access Spirit's attention—asking.

S - Spirit recognizes your intention—seeking.

K - know Spirit supports your request—knowing.

Access Spirit's Knowing—to manifest your intention. "Guide me into this intention; show me the steps to take; teach me how to do this." There is ample time for each step in these endeavors. This all keys back to responding to God in service, the ultimate joy of every being of Creation. This is a primary law of Creation—serve yourself by responding to others, serve others by responding to yourself. Abundance will always follow unselfish service, if we realize that everything that is accomplished is for the whole. There is always this interaction. As you continue to embody your divinity this becomes clearer and clearer.

God is your life.

God is the life of everything.

The term God has been watered down, so to speak, from its origins. "God created the heavens and earth"[19] is the statement—different than the generally held idea that "this god that I know created the heavens and earth." The flowing concept of God has been referred to by numerous names among the human factions during Earth history. These ideas have changed and grown through the ages as various interpretations surface and collide. We suggest that even now, there is little openness to expanding the terminology. Within most minds the hearing of the word 'God' brings memories to surface that are connected into mass consciousness, therefore it is helpful to use expanded terms. Other words surface in this attempt that work together to suggest a new conscious comprehension. Please realize there is no intention to separate aspects of Creation with these words; it is to open the door, by-passing the guard of personality confinement. Intend to let go of stereotypes—even of God—and ask for a new understanding of Creation energies.

Possibilities equal limit-less-ness. Broaden your scope by inviting assistance with being all that you can be in every moment, in every activity, every feeling, every thought, thus allowing continual expansion of Spirit vibrations. You become the heir of God, the embodiment of the inherent Goodness of Creation. Asking stimulates assistance, seeking activates imagination, knocking opens the physical realm for manifestation. "Ask, and it shall be given you; seek, and ye shall find; knock, and it shall be opened unto you."[20]

*My God who art in my heart*
*I honor Your Presence.*
*Manifest through my life the Essence creating my being*
*In life without as it is within Thee.*
*With every moment is my abundance fed with Love.*
*Transform me with Thy Love in all levels and situations.*
*May I see Thy Beingness in every encounter as I share*
   *this Love.*
*Let my Being move through others in the ecstasy of life*
   *within Your fold,*
*For from within my heart, when filled with Your Presence,*
*Thy Love transforms my doing into the flowing of Love*
   *Essence from Thy Glory and Divine Self.*
*With gratitude and devotion, I honor Your Presence*
   *forever and ever. Amen.*

# 15 Meditation to Connect with Guides and Personal Angels

YOU MAY CHOOSE to activate or increase your awareness of personal Guides and/or Angels who are willing to assist you with your intentions. They are available consistently without invading personal choices. It is our intention that calls them.

Sit comfortably and breathe out any tension, any concerns. ✺

Notice the body as it relaxes completely, feeling safe and secure. ✺

Connect your awareness to your heart. ✺

Feel your heart connect with Earth. ✺ ✺

Set your intention to connect into your Soul energy at the fastest possible frequency available at this time. ✺ ✺

Now open your imagination to the many dimensions that are within and around you at this moment. ✺

Include the physical bodies our Spirits inhabit, bodies unseen by our physical eyes.

Let's imagine there is an energy Spirit that lives with any plants that are around. Devas are those who assist the plant kingdom. Each plant has one. ⊛

And there is other unseen life within the area. There may be Spirits of ancient civilizations who remain or who use this geographic area periodically, ⊛

Or a guide or guides overseeing this present activity. ⊛

Call your HigherSelf and the Light, represented by your individual reality to be present—Christ, Sanadra, Buddha, Divine Mother, Archangels and Masters. ⊛ ⊛

Ask your HigherSelf to assist with your intention to meet your personal guide. If you have experienced one previously, you may ask that this energy connection be intensified. ⊛

Create or go to a place that is special for you, a space of comfort and support. ⊛ ⊛

Gradually turn your perception 360 degrees to experience all surroundings. ⊛ ⊛

In the distance there is an area of color different from any of the surroundings.

Experience how this color intensifies as it moves closer. It radiates a feeling of love, joy and protection. As it moves closer, it begins to take form. ⊛ ⊛

Perceive how this Being looks, how It feels. Notice how you feel in this Presence. ⊛

Understand who this Being says It is. If you choose, ask for a name to satisfy your mind. ⊛ ⊛

Notice how comfortable you feel. If you are not quite

comfortable, ask your HigherSelf to tell you what you can do to feel safe. ✹ ✹

Is there a message for you? ✹ ✹

Do you have questions? Ask and listen for answers, paying attention to every sensation and/or thought. ✹ ✹

This Guide has a special place to show you. Give this Being the freedom to transport you in any manner It wants. ✹

The destination is a beautiful flowing river of crystal water in a setting that is very pleasing to you. Pay attention to the details of the area—the landscape, sky, colors, sounds, smells, feelings. ✹ ✹

Notice an area of sand sloping gently into the water. Feel your Guide leading you to this water—a place so pleasant and safe. ✹

Beautiful Angelic Beings are waiting for you. Feel their presence. ✹

They lovingly lead you into this stream. The warm water feels effervescent and your skin tingles. ✹

While your Guide watches over you, the angels completely bathe you, gently caressing your body with total acceptance and love. Be aware of feelings—tactile and emotional. ✹ ✹

Do you notice tones or singing? ✹ ✹

As they finish, you are escorted to shore and dried with cloud-like towels. ✹

You are clothed in beautiful garments. Experience yourself being cared for so lovingly by these angels. ✹ ✹

Is there anything these Guides have to show you? ✹

Any other place? ✹ ✹

Any other dimension? ✹ ✹

You can ask any questions you wish. ✹ ✹

Ask for a signal that they will use to contact you, different from your HigherSelf signal. It may come as a feeling, a physical sensation, a picture, a word or sound. ✹ ✹

It is time for these Beings to return you to your special place where you first contacted them. Experience this space of comfort and support. ✹

Express your gratitude. ✹

Know that they will return with you to consciousness, always being available to assist when you ask. They never interfere except in rare instances of life threatening situations. They are your Guides, always in loving support of your humanness.

Set your intention to remember all that has happened. ✹

Return your attention now to your physical body and surroundings, noticing feelings and sensations. ✹

Breathe from your heart into Earth and back to your heart. ✹ ✹

Take a couple deep breaths as you return your attention to your body position and support. Slowly and gently move the fingers, feet, legs and begin to stretch. ✹

Open your eyes to be aware of your surroundings, gradually becoming totally conscious of where you are and how you feel, remembering all you have experienced. ✹ ✹ ❀

# 16  Interactions of Life

DURING AN INCARNATION we come here with those others who will care for and stimulate us, as well as those who will push our buttons. These components are represented in every experience and encounter. We can be our own caretaker and stimulator and be involved in any situation from a point of centeredness and empowerment. Embodying this experience and moving into the next adventure leads this discovery of ourselves. As we become comfortable with situations we become mentors for others navigating similar ventures in their stream of life. Each of us can recall times when we had very close relationships with people who are no longer part of our life. We engagedone another as assistants to support activities or as triggers for self-growth. Holding on to any of these people keeps one stuck in that place, unable to ascend into what could be next. It is frequently painful to continue to be awash in these remnants rather than continuing in the stream of consciousness growth.

It is very valuable to know when to let go and move. No sense in grinding corn that is already ground. When you spend time in association with a group of people, say a work situation or club or class, there will be those to whom you are attracted and those with whom you have little contact. There is nothing wrong with this picture. You can be friendly, attentive to all and still be more closely associated with certain people. Do not fret because someone chooses to leave you alone. At this time you has nothing that either stimulates him or her or s/he have nothing to learn from you and vice versa. Welcome those with whom you do have interactions, particularly those who present challenges. These are the ones to focus on. Recall when you thought you were stuck in such a situation. Did their actions or lack of action trigger you? How did you feel? Know that when you have issues with people or things, there is more to experience within such arenas. Running away will not serve you. In fact, there is no running away. This card is on the top of your deck and must be played for your game to continue smoothly. Set your intentions to deal with each encounter as it is given to stimulate ascension—the evolution of your present experiences into Presence. There are always supporters within any 'enemy' camp, so be prepared to allow assistance in while you strengthen yourselves by facing the challenge full forward. When you complete this one, another exciting adventure surfaces.

Self-responsibility opens one to the space of accepting that there is something to learn in every encounter. Look for and welcome the triggers. Be in your truth moment to moment to delve into what is there for you, experiencing every layer, completing this phase so you can be true to yourself in the next. Forget the past. Welcome the present of this moment. Let friends move on and if they should surface again in your life or you in theirs, know there is something pertinent for each of you in this present. Stay out of the story of the past. Welcome who you are in this situation, knowing you have something for one another. It is similar with those with whom you have daily contact. Unless you are in tune with the energy of the moment, you will experience these people as the last time you saw them. You do not know what has happened in the minutes since being together. Even understanding there is no time does not yet alter your last experience of one another. Right now is a new experience. Every moment is *new*. Accept each encounter with respect—the respect you have for yourself. Regardless of the energy presented, it is for you learning about you—how you act and/or re-act from mind's memory. Use these gifts wisely. Great leaps of consciousness are made with amazing results when you attend to every moment with awareness. ✦

These messengers of Divine Essence continually open new pathways for my inspiration and guidance. As the spirals of energy are incorporated within personality, changes are made in our day-to-day lives. We respond from a new place within our heart, which changes the illusionary scope of old beliefs. Change occurs in the areas where blame was held for this or that and we choose to no longer blame ourselves. As we are involved in transformation, we may not realize this detail by detail, however when we broaden our vision we can feel the difference. Notice your perception, the general outlook and the particulars in your life during the past days and weeks. Consider that the actions of those people around you reflect your own changes; they depict your inner feeling—recognized and unrecognized. People show respect; we respect ourselves. We like to be with ourselves; people like to be with us.

When someone does move into blame by seeing anything as your fault, watch your own reactions—take truthful responsibility or leave it. Rather than join in their creation, repeat their words back to them or share another aspect of the idea, being aware that in discussion is the discovery to evolve beyond blame.

Assume responsibility for what is in your life and your interpretation of such encounters from a heart-integrated space. Ask yourself, "How can I be in this place of interaction and keep my heart energy present? How can I do my part to assist this encounter into its faster vibration?" Your heart-centered assistance may seem unwanted. Stay conscious in personal integrity. Make decisions while being responsible to yourself. "What is the loving thing to do?" becomes the question.

Many times when you feel that another is in constant negativity and you find no connection to your present Self, it is time to move out of that experience. Should there be anything that is still represented within your field, it will be brought back to you. The number one decision is to take care of you. There is no way to fix another. When either of you is ready for this energy representation to transform, personal truth will release the hold without arguing or upset beyond the basic encounter. Truth will set you free when holding is unhooked. Move on when you have a clear signal from your internal Self that it is unproductive to remain in the energy. Do not invalidate yourself by becoming a sacrifice or martyr. If the mirror is cracked no one will see clearly. Take a breather to refresh, then re-enter the situation from a more centered space, again checking your own reactions.

The heart exudes personal truth and clearing happens. It could take awhile to locate this heart energy when triggers are firing. Verbalize the truth of the moment and the next truth of that moment, continuing until the doors are opened into the heart of the matter. Follow your HigherSelf in and out of each experience. If at times it seems like you are on a circular route, examine the loop to sense truth, allowing the energy to spring open into a spiral. Growth is your choice. You can keep repeating the same circles as long as you want, even creating chains of circles, never letting go of the past, using each of those to create the next. Or you can choose to open the present link to spiral your life into the richness available. Bless each of the people you encounter, appreciating the gifts you have exchanged, honoring one another's chosen path, knowing that if you have other gifts for one another the spiral will bring you together again.

Your every expression is an interpretation of *I Am* and the personality traits expressed within your blueprint. It is your make-up, you could say. Just as with any physical item, this make-up can be changed. A person can choose to make changes similar to using a cosmic eraser. You are the Cosmic Force. You are the God Force. You are All That Is. Literally! Search every experience, every encounter, every *Being* for the I Am, that part of every thing that is the very same as you—no different. Again, *there is no difference.* ❁

Every aspect of us has a physical residence, a place of contentment, where we feel fulfilled. Until we are ready to be respondable (able to respond), to consciously hold our divinity within the physical realm, some other structure holds it, e.g. a church, a place in nature, a person. Empowerment supports our being our own container, an especially prepared Divine receptacle. Within the whole structure are many resonating chambers or wombs (organs), holding various aspects of our *Beingness*. Energetically there are chambers referred to as chakras, holding individual unique interpretative characteristics. Each is a chalice, molded and held by the feminine, filled by the male aspect. Complete filling of Divine Love may take several lifetimes. As energy is continually received and held in a Source/Heart/Earth connection, the chalice does fill and overflows to share universally. This flow continues as long as there is receivership for our personal Divinity. If this stops, the chalice level drops to sustainable levels, however, continuing to give depletes the internal sup-

ply. Optimal flow continually expands the vessel and the outpouring of compassion in this flow of love supports others without attachment as they learn to fill their own vessels. As we clean
and polish ourselves, removing old patterns, we open these places
for heightened revelations about our spirituality. In meditation
ask HigherSelf to expose your chalice.

I first saw this chalice in a meditation I was leading. It supported the group energy, creating a container to hold the expressions of each participant. It appeared as a brilliant receptacle,
elevated on a tower within a Light column with energy flowing
from both ends. Its feeling was one of providing a womb to integrate human and Spirit and Earth. I noticed that every person
had this same form within his or her field. In some it appeared
to hold them, in others it appeared within their physical body.
There were vessels partially filled, some with holes, others over-
flowing, some were grounded, others floating. I was intrigued
with these formations, asking to be taught about the various conditions.

What you are seeing reflects the individual's ability to receive. There are those who continually
give without taking time to replenish. To be at
one's maximum energy level, consciousness needs its
Source flow. When your container is filled you can operate
at full stream. There are several ways to manage this. Sleep
is a natural space for filling, however, frequently the morning's activities are all give, give, give, thus depleting the sup-
ply. Effective use of meditation is another natural venture
for replenishing yourself. Ask to be shown your chalice. See
its condition and ask for guidance about clearing, using
HigherSelf's teaching about receiving as one of the tools for
cleansing and filling.

It is vital to become aware of how one invalidates reception. Genuinely examine habits that revoke gifts, whether

verbal or physical. Intend to be attentive to receive graciously, being cognizant of all associated feelings. Experience receiving as actively as giving and you are well on your way to having your chalice overflow.

All experiences occur to instigate interaction between participants. We move from this engagement to another, sometimes at personality direction, sometimes with our inner knowing. Regardless of the depth of connection, each gives and receives, preferably without attachment to outcomes. We can support others, encouraging their creativity without any agenda by not doing the work for them. Otherwise we initiate playing into whatever drama is presented. As their ideas and ways of accomplishment change, it is our choice to fit into the new pattern or not. At times proposals from others overshadow our own creativity.

We choose how to interact from present integrity when energies become uncomfortable. Our interpretations do not mean something is wrong with their picture. It is an indication of some jarring in our experience. Each participant can examine how the current affair is or is not serving them and make personal choices as to the validity of their involvement. Caroline Myss[21] talks of times when Spirit presents a direction for our lives that we seem to ignore and if we continue to do so, Spirit intervenes by putting us through the fire, so to speak, to bring clarity about our continued evolvement. In looking at many past events from where I am now, I see how this has occurred in my life. I recognize the improbability of my being where I am presently—physically and emotionally and spiritually—without all of the seeming interference from thoughts about where and how I wanted to be. And sometimes even such realization is uncomfortable. Every experience is an opportunity to feel whatever performance of anger, sadness, grief and/or love, compassion, or forgiveness seems appropriate in order to integrate a new level.

In this way, every experience is incorporated into empowerment within Self, increasing concentrations of divinity. Continual movement while loving myself is one of my intentions.

Until I was a sophomore in high school I was always at the end of the line because my name began with a W, or on the back row because I was taller than anyone in my class—including male classmates. My mother was very conscientious about reminding me to 'hold my shoulders up.' I bless her for this. We continued this exchange as long as I lived at home. Years later my voice coach asked me to hold my shoulders back. My habit of holding my shoulders up jumped right in. The coach said, "No, not that way. Pretend there is a string pulling from your top thoracic vertebra straight up. This straightens your spine while *relaxing* the shoulders." This was a totally new concept about posture. Maybe it had been said before, but this was the first time I had heard it. Almost forty years after Mother's reminders, I got it. In reality this is a slight modification in shoulder position. Energetically there is a huge difference. Before I was always holding myself up. Through the years, other energies decided I could also hold them up, thus placing more 'on my shoulders.' As I have incorporated this new stance I am relaxed within myself while my life reflects my more balanced structure.

There are many things we do or think that are slightly off-kilter to our optimum point of balance. In any moment we can alter our consciousness a tiny bit to discover another reality. It is as if we are a stream, moving across the meadow of life, around rocks and boulders, within banks that have 'always' been there. One day a child comes along to play, moves a rock and our flow is different. Because of what the coach said, I rearranged a thought pattern, creating a new awareness that feels better and seems much more pleasing in my energy field. With this new consciousness I am training my body to respond to a new stance, letting go of 'stuff' that is unproductive in my present life.

I have discovered other nuances in my habits and thoughts

that, when examined and rearranged, more fully serve present intentions—such as defining the term 'work.' I wondered about the energetic difference and similarity with work and play. There was the context that if it's work there is pressure, distaste and reluctance within its structure. We frequently hear the term "I have to go to work," usually accompanied with the energy of "It's not what I want to do, but I have to." Rarely is there excitement. Why not? Enthusiasm is a valuable aspect of anything we enjoy. What gives with work? Okay, we have to work to receive pay so we can purchase necessities. Is it possible for this to be fascinating—an expression of our grandeur in relationship to others while each of us engages our creative expression? What would it take to skew our attitude about work so it can be rewarding, reassuring, cooperative? It can be just a nudge into another realization of our worth—primarily to ourselves and from this place, sharing with others. For me, work has become fun—most of the time.

It takes connection to your heart to fulfill your creative expression in everyday events. You have spent so much time ignoring yourself so that others will find you valuable, so that you will fit on the team, be paid more, be respected. All of this is asking something outside yourself for your reality. As you move into consciousness of your own divine nature, that you are the creator of your experiences—everyone with whom you have contact feeds you patterns of exactly what you are feeding yourself. If this is doubt, then the boss will doubt that you can head up the new department. If it is judgment, everyone on the committee will question the steps you have outlined as the most competent way to complete the task. If you insist on controlling your world, your employees will be disgruntled, rebellious and dissatisfied. When you are aware of your own capabilities—and shortcomings—you attract those who have similar ideas, as well as those who can fill the vacant places necessary for the total creation of something evolutionary, worthwhile and beautiful.

Refrain from censuring your attitudes towards others until you look within. How are you blaming yourself for the present scene? Do you admit there are things you would rather not do? Can you express your truth to allow someone else to step in with that expertise? You can give directions forever; however, unless you consider suggestions, you will continue to re-create past events. Stop. Open to introspection. Meditate, listening to the voice within that knows exactly what can be accomplished in the present moment. Receive. Move forward one moment at a time without attempting to move the pebbles. Be the flowing stream. Know your banks will overflow in the perfect moment creating new pathways for your energy. Stand tall, sit straight and focus on the intention to *be* while all the pieces are being placed in order. Realign your thoughts to include the fun of discovery, of creation, order and chaos—whatever is presented. Flow with it in awe of the power and creativity of freedom. Stay in the flow of this moment until that inner message gives another direction. ✸

For a while we lived in an apartment where two units had a common porch. A cosmetic upgrade to the complex entailed new paint on all outside surfaces, including the porch floors—a pleasing change. After one of my trips out of town, I noticed what appeared to be dried liquid spills marring the porch surface. After a couple weeks, choice seemed to dictate a live-with-it-or-clean-it-up decision. It was interesting to watch my vacillating thoughts surface. One question was about when to perform my task—while the neighbors were or were not at home? I looked at what motive was active. How could they let this mess be here so long? Would they feel reprimanded because I was cleaning up after them? If they saw me doing this, would they realize their sloppiness? Or would they even notice? My personality hooked into doing the job right. The facts are: I cleaned the porch on my timetable, and, unknown to me at that time, someone was at home.

The experience was rewarding for me in that there was excitement as I played barefoot in the sudsy water. An opportunity had presented itself for my joy—or my upset. I let upset go and had fun with the process of swishing away judgment, needing to do it right, and wondering what someone would think. I was thrilled at the results when I later opened my door to greet a floor that looked newly painted. It made no difference what they thought. I was given an opportunity to see how my personality hooked into my performance and someone else's lack of performance. Choosing to enjoy the process transformed personality energies of judgment, allowing the freedom to honor my choice beyond emotional entanglement.

We are responsible for our reality around and in any situation. We are out of alignment if we react in any way other than love, politeness, compassion and mercy for all interactees. Reaction is something within, to notice and examine. Any intention for growth connects with these experiences, for-gives us for engaging with judgment/control/fear and moves us into the space of love. In this particular incident I collapsed the sphere of love at first, deactivating compassion when I moved into judgment as I looked at the stained porch. Then I used the opportunity for giving love to all involved and for-giving myself love for being out of acceptance to what was. I asked for continued support to realign possibilities.

Whatever we notice outside ourselves has an aspect within. Reactions such as control, offense, and withdrawal pinpoint repressed energies tending to run our lives. Freedom comes if we notice these mirrored aspects as being presently active and we consciously choose another way to express ourselves in the moment, apart from personality patterns. Recognizing ego responses that are running our lives is a step to freedom and gives us an opportunity to act beyond any judgment, regret or disappointment. It is when we grab any ego reaction and hold it that we move into past or future—out of *Now*. Even to say "I shouldn't feel..." is to get out of now, implying that God is incorrect in creating this moment. *Now* is creating newness every moment without anything other than Isness.

# 17 The Tides
## of Nature's Subsistence

EVERY BEACH holds a fascination for me—from barren sand to rocky cliffs. I have learned to fully explore it now for the next tide may wash, hide or remove whatever has been uncovered or deposited. The ocean has its way with these things. One day the sand is smooth with nothing apparent; the next there are hills and valleys, many objects or nothing. Its continual surprises draw my interest. There is a wonder on the beach in early morning, when there are no other human footprints. I accumulate experiences rather than specimens, exploring, finding, examining and leaving things for the waves to caress or for others to discover.

One late afternoon I found such tranquillity upon a wide span of Oregon beach. The temperature was perfect; sea gulls lazily soared the air currents, diving in high gear when spotting a morsel. I was within *me* as I walked along. In my peripheral vision I noticed something glistening in the sunlight. There was a bubble about two feet across forming a sphere of rainbows in its interaction with the sun. Then there were more. What delight! The source was on top of the high bank where a lady was creating these magnificent forms with a bucket of solution and a large bubble maker. The bubbles moved with the breeze, slowly descending, sitting momentarily before dissolving into rainbow puddles on the sand. The colors lingered as the moisture slowly dissipated. Others drifted to the sea, floating briefly before merging. Elements of creation in operation.

There are so many parallels in your world—taking something to create something else. God is everything needed for the creation of any idea you can envision. Ideas materialize when all elements are ready, just as the lady on the bank was an ingredient for your bubbles of joy. Minds do peculiar things in their wondering 'if.' Consider the species of mosquitoes whose eggs lay dormant for decades until the rainfall is perfect for their growth. The same with seeds in dry climates—those that only bloom after a certain amount of rain. They grow, mature, seed and become dormant until all elements support their growth again—flowers, insects, viruses and bacterial strains. The absence of only one element interrupts manifestation. You witness this all around you every day. Your car doesn't run if one small item is missing or out of alignment. Leave the yeast out of bread baking and you get something else. Split an atom one way to connect to its nucleus and electrons; change the structure for an explosion. One aspect of a healthy cell mutates forming disease. Supplying another element makes a different change. The interrelationship between the whole and any other component is evolution in progress.

Any purpose is served for the required amount of time that any one tiny element needs to makes an ever so slight change in the present creative process. After many unions these mutations become evident—another form is present. Continual creation. There is no stopping here or there. Check in—you know the feeling of having everything complete, when there seems to be nothing except your present experience of creation—your life.

❧

While paying attention to your internal messages, consciously consider the following:

What would be different if you were continually aware of change?

Conscious of always being in a space for newness?

In the interaction of re-creating something from what was?

In allowing and supporting the ebb and flow of something new with every breath—physically, emotionally and spiritually?

Why does anyone want to continue to repeat and repeat…repeat…repeat?

Not creating is a space of nonexistence—impossible.

The motion of Source cannot be stopped.

Your thoughts are creation in process.

You can never think the same thing twice.

Recall a past experience; every time the scene comes forth, thoughts are different.

One time you may recall the colors; another time you may recall senses, faces, ideas, varied emotions. However, each remembrance is different. ❧

So it is with all endeavors. Holding on to any particular part is like trying to drive your car with the gearshift in neutral. There is no returning to the past. That is the way Creation was. Now is always the time of birthing. Tomorrow is for the manifestation of what is being put forth in this moment—mutating differently from your conjured ideas.

You can build a brick wall to support your garden. Every brick has in its own moment of placement, held together with bonding you mix from elements. When finished you look at the wall and recall the experience as a whole rather than distinguishing each movement it took to accomplish this project. And while you were building, other developments were unfolding. Within a predetermined length of time the moisture you put in the cement interacted with the bricks to form a bond to hold all in place. Now, what would have happened if you had not used any water? The bonding material would have been dust to be blown here and there, thus becoming evolution with a totally different result. If rains had soaked the bricks, a greater length of time would have been required for the proper interaction to strengthen the bond. To successfully form a brick wall certain elements have to be used in correct proportions. So it is with every experience you have. Something left out creates a different scenario. Clear intention assists one to focus on the steps needed for certain outcomes. Other experiences may be totally 'with the wind' in that one is willing to participate without knowing any details.

The wall wouldn't manifest without the builder. You would not be present in bodily form without two people to begin your form. You are both the created and the Creator. You are created in the imaging of God just as a sperm and egg uniting is this imaging. The brick wall is Creation 'in form from imagination,' existing in the experience of unifying its parts for as long as its service is appropriate. Then it changes to something else—returns to its individual ingredients or is re-created into another sculptural aspect. Everything does its job and moves on. So with the bubbles interacting without consciousness of their beauty—creating form for their lifespan.

Air and water are examples of nature's fluid expressions. Storms bring ferocity altering the landscape of earth, water and sky. In their fury they sometimes cleanse and other times regurgitate from the depths items stored for centuries. Obstructions within their path act in resistance. A syncopation of air, water and matter rearrange elements in creative production. Be as a tree swaying in any interaction, as dirt becoming mud; be ready to receive the onslaught while adjusting to the flow. As an awesome expression of Creation with no attachment to what was, our lives can run free.

I've experienced one illustration of this freedom while sitting on the bottom of the ocean where sea fans and soft sponges swayed and schools of fish moved around my body with no apparent recognition of my being a foreign object. The sea world continued its activity without interruption or my intervention. I am aware that in my world there are things I do not see; my focus can become so narrow that I fail to see the whole. And at other times I am so in touch with the intangible aspects of humanity and nature as to feel totally connected.

I recall the wedding of a friend's son—at dawn on the beach. Most of the participants came from inland to celebrate this creation of matrimony. The atmosphere vibrated with their love for one another. The normal beachside morning was not disturbed. Sea gulls soared in pursuit of breakfast. Waves accompanied the flutist. Earth moved for the sun to rise out of the ocean, dispersing the morning clouds in a blaze of color. The dawn's sacredness enveloped and supported the moments of union—with nature and people. Were more than footprints left as we exited the sand? Creation moved on. The experience touched us individually and collectively. Another celebration of life. Everything evolved due to the willingness of each element's presence. We came together, we created, and we dispersed to create anew.

Is anything else even possible? In one exercise I examined the energy of destruction. I explored creating, being and forming, and found when any of this was 'destroyed' every element was still present to be reformed into another circumstance or object. All That Is creates from Its total perfection and in Creation, there can be no destruction. Essence creates and then recreates that creation into another creation. Look at how we do this creation/dis-creation thing in our lives. We build, re-structure; we burn wood for heat; we devour food for energy. We only change the appearance of our world. Destruction is not an option—evolution prevails.

Creation is everything—from floating in tranquil water to being pushed and tossed in the ravages of a storm. Sitting in the twilight, campfires, dozing with sounds of nature to lull one to sleep. Skiing down hills or across water. Watching soaring eagles or gliding pelicans. Filled with wonder about the kaleidoscopic shapes and colors or creating havoc to dis-create present life forms. Life is evolving, restructuring, sustaining, mutating within individual and collective creation.

Awareness of your importance in the whole assists in what man would term balanced creation. Mass consciousness has valuable concepts about how creation should unfold, however there are places where individuality plays a gigantic role in the path of evolvement. Your influence comes into play primarily in making self-assessment adjustments to past incidents. You learn to alter intrusions into your emotions and beliefs to facilitate awareness that patterns need not be repeated unless you choose to reenact the past. You become aware of a schism in the field of energy and allow your CreatorSelf to smooth out the wrinkle so that your present is altered.

Now the same technique is used in regard to your outside world. You choose friends to reflect experiences to smooth out various wrinkles. You do this with your employment, your social groups, your neighbors and partners, even your children. This same scenario occurs within the evolvement of your planet. A group comes together to work on a cause that each perceives as valuable for the continuation of human life. However, in another part of the world, people disagree with your tenets and efforts to persuade them to live per your ideologies. You judge their lives by your standards. Their reality is being disavowed. They resent intrusion, particularly if it means they cannot follow their collective culture. People live the way they do because it is their choice. 'This is the way we have always done it' does not make it so for everyone. Neither does someone insisting upon change. There is no right and no wrong way for any one or group.

Love is the only element that can create nondisruptive change. There are organizations that foster change by physically demonstrating other possibilities. For instance, a major hiccup occurs when the food chain is interrupted. Sometimes people become ill after eating seafood—a staple in many parts of the world. Gradual alterations in the quality of life-sustaining elements enforce slight mutation in the physical make-up of people, enabling local conditions to support a quality of life. Rapid change brings immediate shifts such as disease. This interaction in life-supporting components may instigate someone's envisioning an opportunity to assist with ideas to cleanse the toxicity. One gathers people, supplies and necessities to install an updated piping system rather than have water run in an open ditch. Up until now, no one in the that particular area had such an idea nor did they have any pipe, therefore that option was unavailable. Now, if the assistants' motives are for personal gain, the project is set for failure. If they are willing to help without rewards, the project's success is guaranteed—giving and receiving without attachment. Mass consciousness of the need for clean water is sustained. Upgrading the

components of health and hygiene supports society's evolution.

Creation has many forms that are invisible to your personality's eyes, yet available for you to experience when
you allow yourselves to explore beyond the obvious. Your
tide of involvement rises and falls exposing attributes of
your interest—some to be picked up and others to leave for
another time. You can effortlessly swim with all possibilities
contained within the natural checks and balances in the
scheme of evolution. All operable energies of Earth are to be
honored. Consider your lives a vast sea holding all potential
available for sequential disclosure according to your willingness to float freely while riding whatever waves are
formed by the interaction of All That Is ✸

> Be Authentic
> As the Ocean
> As Nature
> In the Moment

# 18  From Trying to Flowing

Trying is the mind distracting us out of our present situation into attempts to make something happen. Trying never moves anything; either we do it or we don't. This need to change something reflects a personal doubt in God's plan, that we have a solution or we know better than God. It is as if we say this needs to be another way rather than accepting the moment as perfect. Sure, we notice the moment is happening this way and our mind shows us it could be another way, however this is reality right *Now*. And nothing we think can change this moment. In the next moment we can adjust our posture, change our location or look at things differently—but that is in the next moment.

You put so much stock in what you can see and what you can do as if there is something to change. You move the rocks and build bridges. Some alter the stream, some sit on the bank, others wander around within, and a few of you go with the flow. Take the plunge and become the flow regardless of what this seems to look like. Ride the waves, be in the shallows, explore the depths. Check out everything as you become aware of it. This is your *Being* in consciousness and doing from within.

You may notice that when this is happening, some other

possibility cannot occur where you are. It is not to say all possibilities cannot occur at the same time. Their occurrence is beyond your scope of vision in that moment. At times you want to experience so many things, wanting to be there while you are here, wanting a particular person to be with you when they are somewhere else. In physicality this is impossible; however, if you have the thought you create an energetic connection. Whether they are aware of the dynamics is irrelevant. You can be in more than one place at a time —a natural attribute that is beyond mind consciousness.

Some of you bemoan the fact that you can do only one thing at a time and sense a space of lack when you cannot be available for other events in the same time frame. Possibilities are endless; there are millions of scenarios available to each of you. And yet the path you are experiencing dictates certain avenues for manifestation. This does not mean you lack anything; it is just that right now you are responding to the perfection of this moment that dictates your being here with this experience. Other situations move in their perfection without your involvement. Avoid feeling left out, for whatever interchange is in your life path is there in the perfect timing for your optimum growth experience.

You have the opportunity to acknowledge thoughts, to notice their attachment to your present condition. Why does this thought or emotion surface in this particular situation? Is this something you want to remove from your life? Go fully into feeling any emotion that is playing such a dominant role in your present reality. Does it serve in this moment? If not, ask for clarity as to how to transform it into a faster vibration of love.

As you explore the uniqueness of each experience, you open to total knowing of what is available in this moment, rather than dwelling on what was out of alignment in the moments passed or what might be missed in the next. Within this surrender comes peace with what *Is* present. Devotion to your own experience in each moment is the key. As you become fascinated with unfolding life, you set in motion the patterning for excitement to be present in all moments, thus being a mystical visionary, the Master within. ✹

Whatever is happening is perfect in that each participant has opportunities for introspection and growth. Most of me appreciates every opportunity provided to stimulate my growth. Sometimes my heart hears disreputable energies and is comfortable. Other times I am drawn into personality interaction. Reactions of love and fear surface when a person or entity that has been created in Love is being discredited and misrepresented. We can hold the integrity individually and collectively, while the larger picture opens to show how each perception is unique. It is interesting to notice how my personality often has some comments while calmness permeates my *Being*.

One day I felt disconnected—from my location, from those around me, even from myself. Normal functioning continued without my being conscious of what was happening. I have learned to let myself be just where I am. I was really feeling the blahs. After a period of time I realized there was another aspect of me totally loving the depressing part that was so active. This other piece of me felt like a very loving mother/father energy. It recognized the feelings of discomfort without needing to fix anything, totally accepting that at this moment 'this is the way it is.' It was as if a loving parent were embracing a pouting child, giving permission for the child to be just exactly who it was. I watched in fascination as the disconnected aspect noticed it was being recognized without judgment and its disruptive energy transformed into love for itself. The physical change was very noticeable, moving from sensing oblivion into motivation. Gratitude immediately surfaced bringing tears of recognition of the growth opportunity and my intention to be available to myself with love for all of me.

My years of white-water kayaking taught me about flow, how to be in the rhythm of a current, how to use it in directing my course. Because of the boat's design I could sit centered and guide my passage by leaning this way or that. The 'trick' was being centered in the river's flow. And there were those faster moving rapids where paddles and muscle maneuvered me around obstacles. The ecstasy of matching self with flow whether floating, shooting a rapid, skimming the surface on skies—either behind a boat or downhill—represents feelings associated with living our play in passionate aliveness. Balanced without trying, without any attachment beyond this moment. We set our intentions and follow through with a determination of awareness *as we feel directed*—without pushing or coercing, exerting muscle or leaning one way or the other. When we notice we are out of the stream we can re-route ourselves without attempting to direct the flow. By noticing where we are and following the natural progression of our energy and our attention, we complete these particular energetics and enlarge our capacity to receive and thus we have more to give. When we use these energetics there is no want or desire for anything to be other than the way it is. Need is absent. Living is. Experiencing is.

You hear about moving from dimension to dimension. Energy's fluidity has to be slowed to move into slower/lower dimensions, sped up to be in a faster/higher dimensions. Dimensions can be considered lower or higher since you understand them to a greater degree when we refer to them as 'places,' when in fact everything is right here; there is no 'there.' Since we realize that definition colors individual perception of terminology, our terminology is to assist you with the interpretation of the energy we are presenting. Therefore, for greater understanding, there will be different ways of saying the same thing.

You have watched the swirling of the water as waves move in and through pools, through floating vegetation. You have noticed the swirls in the way the grass has been laid exposed by the outgoing tide. You have noticed rock patterns, the flow of wind through grain fields and orange trees. So it is with your life, your growth and your consciousness. Consider your thoughts as energy moving in 'rhythm' to your present reality. One perceived reality on your plane is that everything happens, stops, begins again. *This is not so.* Synchronization is constant rhythm. Swirls, eddies, pools, action, reaction; all is encompassed in your Essence of Presence. This is real union—flowing with, through, in and out, one avenue into the next, moving through dimensions, planes, realities. There is no way for man to dent this movement. Your ego self thinks it can out-maneuver Creation. Ha! This is one of your fallacies! Everything has its place and its time frame in your dimension. Everything seems to have a beginning and an end. Many of you are beginning to understand absolutes are inconsistent with divine expression.

When one is in this flow, consciousness is steeped with Creation energy. That what you want is not immediately attainable is the result of your intention within the flow of all other inhabitants of Earth—as well as with all of creation. It is not that you cannot have it; it is that the tide has not caught up to that expression. With this understanding you can allow your ego more freedom to live this rhythm more fully. Be in the stream consciously without connection to anything other than your own spiritual journey. Accept that you are unique. There never has been and never will be another you.

All of our in-the-moment living doesn't lessen our responsibility, doesn't mean we can be inactive and accomplish our intentions, that we can lie indifferently on a silver platter or a bed of roses. In this moment it is as it is and the next is coming our way. Awareness of my total surrounding—sounds, sights, feelings, smells—cultivates inspiration, empowering all activities. In choosing to be the truth of our *Being* in every moment perhaps we would live more freely, with greater compassion for ourselves and others. We might be content to work on our own or merge with one another to stimulate possibilities into reality. When movement is unobstructed, everything is nourished with fluidity. When we hear the term 'living on the edge,' I suggest we jump into life completely, into the stream of Infinite Wisdom— the uncharted territory of our unique creation. Each of us does make a difference from the depths of who we are. Know thy self to know God.

In one of his books, Dr. Jacob Liberman says, "Our capacity for full awareness is based on how attentive we are in the present. When we are analyzing rather than feeling our experience, the clarity, energy and passion that we bring to life is reduced.... Yet sages tell us that happiness is simply the ability to fully appreciate whatever is happening now. The more present we are, the more satisfaction, joy and love we can both give and receive."[22]

# 19 Meditation for Monad Activation

THE MORE CONTACT we have with other than our physical selves the easier it is to access Divine Essence. We learn to let go of expectation, to let go of desires, of definitions.

The physical heart is only a tiny aspect of your SpiritualSelf Heart. Remember, the heart is the place of unification, of Divine Love. How could you think your physical self is big enough to be the whole? From the vantage point of the Heart of your Monadic energy, you tap into a far greater Force that moves into infinity, a place for multiple discoveries. Similar to what you perceive as your SoulStar energy container, there is another aspect of God waiting for you to come into the Self-power of Divine Essence. This spiral continues to focus, open and create—focus, open and create.

In this expansion there is a merging with other parts of Self. You become aware of you as an exquisite composite. Experiences erupt, entering another realm, joining the spiraling composite of continual evolution. What is in these realms is beyond comprehension until your vibrations resonate with the next level. Your contemplation and acceptance of this will create an expanded view of possibility. ✸

For me to experience a more conscious sensation of my Monad, my guides showed me another exercise with infinity breathing. This exercise will bring your awareness of the Monadic energy more fully into your fields to facilitate your own growth. Personal healing begins to function from this level, creating a more spiritually grounded focus of energy. As with other meditations, your experience will be enhanced by making a tape in your own voice.

୬

Move into your space of relaxation, a place where you feel safe and loved. ❂

Breathe deeply, inviting your Guardians and supporters to be present. ❂

Move into the space of *Now*, aware of thoughts and let them go. ❂

Let go of all feelings and desires as they surface. ❂

Set your intention to experience the Monad. ❂

Ask your HigherSelf to assist. ❂

Inhale from beyond the Monad into your heart and exhale into infinity. ❂ ❂

Now begin imaging the breath from your personal heart to the Monadic Heart and the Creator Heart, wherever they are for you. ❂

Acknowledge the Essence quality of God. It is who you are. ❂ ❂

We can choose to physically embody a new vibration of love. ❂

Be with your experience of this love. ✿ ✿

The Essence of God rides on the breath. Breathe in this Essence. ✿ ✿

When you feel the body filled with your breath, invite this Essence energy to fill all the fields around the body. ✿ ✿

Open to share this expanded energy with Earth. You might want to visualize and feel your feet in the mud, in a river bottom; feel the grass, hug a tree. Share love with Earth. ✿ ✿

Whatever sensations are happening in your body, just let them be. Let the power of God, of Divinity, of All That Is be present. Realize that no one has to do anything for this to happen. It is a matter of setting your intention, sensing the breath. Come into a space of stillness, into the nothingness. It happens. ✿

Choose to open your heart to the Essence even more. ✿

Notice anything that creates a fear of love. ✿ ✿

Continue opening to Earth, the home you have chosen at this time. ✿

Feel Earth's support, its love. ✿

Move your attention to a hand's length above your head, to the SoulStar. Allow the breath to be like a slide for Divine Essence as It enters your body through the top of your head. ✿

Now take your attention to the Monadic energies in the 12th chakra, approximately your height above your head. ✿

Begin inhaling from the Heart of the Monad into the back of your heart, out the front of your heart and into the center of Earth. ❀ ❀

Exhaling from this Earth center, up into the back of the heart, out the front all the way to the Monad. ❀ ❀

Imaging your breath following this figure 8, inhale the energies from the Heart of the Monad down through your heart all the way into Earth, and exhale up through your heart into the Monad. ❀ ❀

If you find this circuit expanding beyond these places, let it happen. Let it be whatever it is. You are using the breath to pull faster frequencies of your own Essence into physicality. ❀ ❀ ❀

Letting everything be just as it is, keeping the breathing pattern going, watching with imagination. ❀ ❀

Be attentive to the physical body, noticing any feelings, any sensations—any pictures, sounds, colors. ❀ ❀ ❀

Whatever thoughts pop into mind, welcome them as part of right now, this divine moment, asking the mind to record all that is happening. ❀ ❀ ❀

(You can choose to stop the tape here for a longer experience.)

Bring your attention to your heart and consciously breathe a circle from your heart into the Earth and back to your heart. ❀ ❀

Set your intention that the next three deep breaths return your attention to your physical position, support and location. ❀ ❀

Slowly and gently move your fingers, feet and legs and begin to stretch. ✹

Open your eyes, keeping them defocused as you begin to be aware of your surroundings. ✹

You can set the intention to hold these feelings and this quietness as long as you choose. ⬲

# 20  Accepting Transmissions

Light transmissions are powerful expansions of vibrational energy, a downloading of greater dimensions of our CosmicSelf entering into our physical realm. As ideas that seem to be polarities come into balance, we embody our own sovereignty. Enlightened healing follows guidance into and through every process as unconscious wisdom emerges. Expanded awareness holds the sacred atmosphere of passionate Divine Wholeness.

During such transference, profound informational concepts bring new dimensions to life. Acceptance and embodiment of these transmissions are magnificent connections into faster frequencies. Ministers are usually unaware of one very important aspect of the expanding consciousness phenomenon. Biblical text refers to 'washing with the Holy Spirit.' As healing progresses, definite sensations are activated beyond what we know as ordinary experiences. Physical stimulation such as the quickening of breath and the heart rate, trembling and lack of balance are the results of Light infusions—of Spirit washing through the physical vehicle. Unless these energies are invited to complete their cycle from Spirit through the heart into Earth, this washing is temporary. Consciously connect to Earth for the ultimate experience, feeling every sensation of any transmission. This realigns and balances Divine Essence at the cellular level. Integrated transmissions are a major force in one's reality, changing inter-actions with all else that exists.

Conscious connection to the energy of this complete togeth-erness catapults one into expanded self-awareness and self-expression, awakening life's passion. It alters the way we experience life, changes past behavior patterns, giving us differ-ent solutions to everyday activities. From here we can become a models of empowerment. What happened before now is history. We move into unique places within ourselves while connected to the whole. Spiritual energetic waves accelerate our vibration which, in turn, change our action and perception and the way we engage with others.

At first it is very difficult for the narrow scope of mind to understand these infusions—maybe there's no way it can. When we use heart-centered imagination we can envision our Selves as multidimensional aspects of God Creator within the context of humanity—as Spiritual Beings doing human things. From here our minds seem to accept feelings of Spirit with little need for understanding. My willingness to expand has brought transmis-sions that defy words. The infusions have literally transformed my perspective of possibilities and have deepened my commit-ment to be with the creation of peace through love.

After a healing session of unwinding an energy lodged in my right shoulder, my field expanded from a deep place within my heart, resulting in a huge opening for my further surrender to God. The transformation was intense; hours later I was still embodying it. I devoted everything I am and have as service to expanding love. After several hours I realized this release had opened space for another issue to surface, this time producing mid-back pain. With the assistance of a facilitator I examined its reality, until reaching an understanding that the services of this energy were no longer needed. In the release an additional transmission occurred. My personal stream to the White Light of God opened. I began to travel in this stream, moving quickly and slowly and quickly into various levels—very difficult to describe. At one point I watched the clockwise swirling of an undulating elliptical stream of White Light. Gradually the division or addition continued moving until my entire field was filled with the colored bands rotating around the center in a complete circle— brilliant white tinged with silver and gold. I rode to a new high. Then from the center a shaft of the Light shot down through me into Earth, sending me into ecstasy and tears, and down on the floor—what I call cosmic orgasm. Hours later the integration of this transmission continued. I was filled with gratitude and peace and a knowing that all is in Divine hands. I let go of needing to know what any of this meant as Jesus shared with me:

You have participated in an elevation that is reverberating into all people with whom you are associated. The longing of your heart for dedication to God brings peace and joy and exposes many to these energies. The nebula you tapped into is always present, however, for now you will remain there only short periods of time. A high level of mastery happens when these energies purify your stream and infuse within your daily existence. For now continue your gratitude.

The heart of a seeker is big enough to contain All That Is, God in Its Wholeness. Open your heart even further, while inviting God to use your life to its fullest—what you call surrender. As you were shown today, for the present, external events and people are always present as 'scheduled.' Your longing will bring other opportunities into rhythm with your service. It is a place of *Being*. Let the doing freely happen, staying centered in each encounter. Feel the vibrations. Know that this is the beginning of a whole new layering of energy. And now rest. ✹

Each one of us is like unto an ocean. We touch many, many

kinds of things. Some float in our energy; some live within our systems. We wash languidly on some shores, while on others, individual energy fields create very turbulent reactions. Life and death are continually within our domain. We are so large, so empowering. We are Creation Itself, in every scope that we can imagine. There is no limit to where we are, to where we can be.

This energy was so vivid, so empowering, so experiential. It engulfed me; it drew me into It and into myself at the same time. It was as if I were bursting and imploding instantaneously, lapping against smoothness while simultaneously raging in torrents against other energies. And yet there was no destruction—only continual support for All That Is happening. Although nothing devastating was occurring, my mind wondered about the consequences. Actively using my mind and fingers to transcribe the words helped me ground the energies. Expansion moved through my field—out, in; down, up; every direction and no direction—none whatsoever. It engulfed and exploded all at the same time.

I was aware of what was happening around me while experiencing all of this. The transmission began when I looked at my feet and realized they were larger than usual. My hands were also huge. This huge energy grew into All That Is. Oh! How we are meant to seize the moments when Spirit comes through. Let nothing stand in our way. Open to possibilities over and over again. My lungs wouldn't hold enough air to get all of the energy into my *Being*. My strength was stretched into larger and larger spheres of energy. I rode the imploding and exploding of the sphere, merging within its framework—nebulous, since there was no containment. And yet it seemed to be there as it flowed into the center… out to the edges… into the center… then out again, with All That Is in all of Creation riding within this sphere. The act of Creation was experiencing Itself as a sphere, moving to Its surface and creating Itself again as the center. There was a rhythm of Creation going into the cells of my heart to activate personal Creation energies. I experienced the images of the whole while concurrently being myself as part of the whole, riding the movement as if everything came and went through my own center. While this was occurring I felt totally coherent and totally in the energy. It swept in and out, flushing my solar plexus, like a flood of water swirling and cleansing throughout the entire center part of my body. The credible energy soothed and refreshed while seemingly furious in Its gentleness—like an astringent on a cut—so full of love. It moved into and incorporated the second chakra with the third—love, grace and joy. The Beingnesss of love to the nth degree.

Thank you for the Essence of Divinity. Thanks for giving me time to eat before we started this. In the past I have experienced the feeling of possibly fainting, although that has never happened. These influxes of energy into our systems take time for incorporation. At this time the support around me was also pure Love, pure Essence—such tenderness, such caring gentleness. I was very aware of merging in my heart. The keenness of my insight seemed greater than before. Each chakra had a similar sphere moving in the same way, with the chakra giving and receiving as the energy moved from the inside to outside and in again. My birth family connected, for within my healing, they also receive. From the first chakra the figure eight moved in and out in a spherical wheel as it connected with EarthCore.

What happened was so clear. At any point I could have said I've had enough. I knew without doubt that I would take no more than my physical body could absorb. My intention to truly receive was paramount. It was inspiring to do this by myself— yet no one is ever alone. Our GodSelf and Guides are always present. My willingness to experience all of me in all dimensions was valid. My consciousness of the transmissions was beyond total comprehension at that time. Awareness heightened to a single focal point so alive in mergence that it brought all reality into One while retaining distinctive attributes. I was told to watch the energy working as various people were escorted into the scene. This Love assisted each of them and their collective agreements.

The primary areas involved were the second and third chakras—with the third as the principal one since its empowerment creates safety for everyone. I felt the pain of others and asked how I could assist without taking on their realities. The reply was to breathe deeply and be aware of my heart connection to Source. As they were exposed to the energy they retreated from my field; I had done all I could do.

Doing this seemed to interrupt the intense flow I was in—not diminishing it but temporarily altering my focus. As I came back into my Self, the flow resumed. I was shown this to understand how we move back and forth from daily experiences to our own sovereign space. It seems we need to mindfully reconnect ourselves using meditation. I consciously anchored the infusions as the Fire of the Cosmos from my Monad into the EarthStar.

I'd heard about the flushing that continues for some time as we go through these downloads of energy. Until this experience I had not grasped the significance of the statement. Prior to this, waves had much less intensity. We are never drained when we reach these frequencies. Willingness and intention are the keys to continuing empowering transmissions, clearings and envelopment. Visualizations will expand and vibrate freely, incorporating into one total connection to everything at a much deeper level.

> ✺ Instantly I become a tree, the sap, the flower, the color, the dolphins, the coral, the clouds, the sunset and sunrise. I become the volcano into the earth's origins, the vent through which this phenomenon extends to the EarthCore. I am the steam rising, the rock being propelled into the atmosphere. I become the seed delivered to a new soil to begin a new forest. The experience is total Oneness, the inclusion of everything. Such

experiences are energies that are familiar. I invite my mind to participate, since it doesn't serve to leave any part out of the experience. ❧

These transmissions bring a new mode of behavior in the way in which I respond to life situations. It may take time for my personality to incorporate what this means. I intend to be patient with myself and ask that from others, even when they know nothing about my situation. Because of the affinity we share, everyone close to me is included in this energy shift, even without their conscious consent. This is one of the attributes of friendship. My intention is to serve Source in whatever capacity It enfolds me in any moment.

# 21 Nature in Life

I DRIVE UP a mountain in western Wyoming, up a road that is cut into the sides of the rolling, climbing terrain. The trees become shorter and farther apart as I shift gears going up and around the curves between the rising heights on one side and eye level tree tops on the other. I pull into a parking place near an indentation in the hills. It's lush green; there must be a creek. I am rewarded by the sound of rushing water and then the sparkle of the sunlight in the water as it dashes over rocks, sticks and plants. The creek seems narrow enough to cross, but when I approach I find the water spreads beyond the 'bank,' into moss and thick vegetation. Some protruding rocks could be stepping-stones when the water level is lower. In the valley there is August drought, the lowest water level of the year in many areas, yet at 7,000 feet, water is plentiful. Before the snow-melt, this stream would be invisible.

Wanting to explore the other side, I scout up and downstream, debating whether to remove my shoes. Nowhere is the creek more than eight to ten inches deep. Testing this place and that, I find some mossy protrusions that support my weight as I hop across. Close to the creek are flowers growing in and out of the water, the smaller ones seemingly from vertical moss-covered rocks. One short stalk has two blossoms that are similar to yellow snap-dragons, another like conical bells about two-thirds of an inch long.

I walk uphill, moving as close to the stream as I can, finding that it frequently seeps under dense vegetation rarely more than eight inches tall. Broken limbs and larger tree trunks fell years ago, crisscrossing the shadowed valley between these hills. Suspended several feet above the stream, they frequently challenge my way. I walk along a whitened trunk over the forest plants, able to change courses wherever another has fallen across or under my log. There are several rushing falls created by rocks or pieces of wood. No silt is being carried to lower altitudes. I see no water insects or fish—just this sparkling glacial melt flowing downhill.

As I climb higher, the creek becomes only a sound, completely covered with plants, flowers and limbs. A type of forest raspberry is turning red, a treat for the animals and birds. Here and there a large hemlock grows close to the creek, creating a clearing with variegated light under its limb-span. The loamy soil exudes the pungent smells of discarded needles and decay.

A squirrel suddenly barks its resounding warning that something different is in the area. I stand very still, aware of it running up the tree several feet before it returns, moving across one of the dead falls, stopping to stare, to bark, and then move back to the tree. It checks out several directions before it seems to accept my being there and quiets its noisy scampering. Larger animals have their own access to the stream along paths, frequently under low limbs and decaying wood.

I move into the edges of sunlight where there are grasses and low bushes, squatting on my heels to look from another perspective. A chipmunk is scampering up a fallen log when it suddenly stops with a squeal, looking intensely at this intruder in its world. It moves as the squirrel did, up and down the log, checking out its choices, coming within a few feet before hurrying down another log to its destination. I relax my gaze, opening to my entire expanse of vision and suddenly notice, about eighteen inches in front of me, the movement of a low branch. Bringing my focus to that point, I search for the creator. The movement continues as something makes its way along the ground. It takes concentration to narrow my focus through the gaps between the leaves to see a small rodent moving with determination. It's checking out every inch of the forest floor, moving twigs and leaves in its path. As it comes into view I notice its sleek, brownish fur. It would be so soft to the touch. From what I can see, it appears to be a forest mouse and yet it acts like an aboveground mole, continually searching under everything. Now it finds something it wants, runs back the way it came about ten inches, stopping to eat the morsel. Returning to its previous place, it rechecks this space before moving on to the next. As it comes closer it is less hidden and I can see tiny ears and eyes. Its tail is quite short. Its nose is the unusual part—it seems to be a type of snout. As it comes within five inches of the end of my shoe it roots under some spruce leaves, actually stretching out its right hind leg as it burrows its snout deeply into the loam. The whole animal isn't more than two and a half inches long and only one leg, with translucent webbing between tiny toes, is visible until it suddenly reverses direction and runs back the way it came. As it returns to the finding place it seems to discover that it is out from under heavy vegetation and quickly runs under dense underbrush. I feel so blessed, so special, to have had the privilege of seeing this specimen of Creation, which I later learned, was a shrew. I sense that it never felt my presence, a confirmation of my being rather than doing.

I realize I have tendencies similar to these forms of nature. My adventuresome nature heightens my sense of observation. Noticing details opens pathways for encountering unusual combinations. Being willing to be shown the unusual activates curiosity. I recall reading that, to Frank Lloyd Wright, communing with the world of nature was a way to enlightenment. Inquisitiveness assists us in accepting possibilities beyond the mind's present conception of reality. Imagination activates the senses of seeing, hearing and intuition. All of these attributes play an important role in compassionate living—assisting, ministering, or healing.

I climb up the fairly steep slope farther away from the creek where denser vegetation grows in the sunlight. I find a grassy, sloping spot on high ground and lie down, absorbing the sounds and scents and sun, soaking in the rays that nourish more than this hillside. In winter this whole shallow canyon is covered with snow higher than my head. Now birds and insects dart here and there, through trees or flower to flower. Interesting how little time it took for a couple of flies to discover my being here. They check out my arms and neck. I remember a friend's awareness that flies are scavengers, that they clean whatever they are on, transforming debris through their being. So I tune into their activities, being open to that possibility. Only when one begins exploring the tip of my nose do I choose to wiggle enough to make it fly somewhere else. Then I am aware of feeling tingles in the vacated area, noticing my thought to identify it as displeasure. It could be aliveness; it could be transformation. Perhaps I can have a different experience if the insect returns. I feel one on my arm. What is the difference? The sensations are similar and yet are not distressful. My nose still tickles.

The warmth of the sun and the sounds of the creek lull me into a space beyond what the flies are doing, into a merging with nature. I sense the strength of the trees, their height and grandeur. I can 'hear' the plants on their journey upward and downward, taking their green leaves and flower stalks to the sun while their roots move solidly into the moist earth beneath the moving water. The sounds of growth, of nourishing, of absorbing carbon dioxide and exhaling oxygen. I wonder if my being here upsets the natural balance of these two elements. I am so aware of God in these animals, plants and trees. One young tree had its top broken off and now six new shoots show ten inches of new healthy green—the instinct to produce itself straight to light. There are logs decaying, reminding me of an earlier meditation into the beauty of decay, the natural evolution of fertilization. My body rhythm continues to slow, pulse and breathe. I enter that familiar space of theta brain waves, closing my eyes to sense all that is around me, still aware of the flies, the babbling stream, the smells of the woods. An imaginative experience from another nature center appears in my consciousness.

I am swinging on a vine that is entangled in tree limbs thirty-six feet above its roots, which grow under other plants on the forest floor. Some plants are thriving in the filtered, mellow light close to the ground. Like this vine, others always reach for light, finding it only above the canopy of treetops. Exhilaration and joy fill me as nature supports and rocks me. I can transport myself into the jungles of the world, into cultures I have not personally experienced. There is acceptance of this mobility while I continue to hold the vine in these woods. I sense the sunlight from above and the shadows below, wondering if we are repeatedly suspended between these qualities during our experience of the whole continuum.

I remember my childhood woods and again experience the devas and fairies. Letting go beyond the obvious opens us to seeing that which inhabits something other than normal experience. I slowly open my eyes in practiced defocusing to discover the overhead limbs are outlined in iridescent neon blue. Carefully I hold my gaze while exploring the area of my peripheral vision, seeing differential color on limbs with needles and bare limbs. Experience has taught me to refrain from shifting my gaze or concentrating too much, otherwise the colors will disappear. With this perception I can see the tree deva, which seems to flow in and out of the tree with colors that are similar to the tree parts although a more vital hue. I image the presence of these Beings and express my gratitude for their continual support for all aspects of this alpine forest. Next to that grandfather spruce is a deva almost as tall as the tree. Others sit under galax leaves; some watch the flowers. It is enticing to experience this other reality.

In the distance I hear a semi, downshifting as it travels down the mountain asphalt. The breeze through the trees keeps me suspended in the silence of this mountain slope, down which the creek is flowing. Time is out of mind. I am part of this slope, part of this particular experience of nature. I am tremendously grateful for being in this space—in this particular expanded space of Beingness, of Oneness, feeling as if there is no reason to ever move from this spot. That somehow if I decide to stay right here, everything will be just fine, just perfect. Innocence sees this instant, the space of real aliveness, of being with what is the moment. I relax into this experience. I open to its unfolding. I wonder how the breeze makes its way through the forest, wonder if when the breeze passes, the energies we call leaves are just as they were before or are they refreshed? Distraught? Relaxed? There is no structure, no restrictions, life here is fullness no matter how humanity defines it. Through its inherent DNA codes, nature mirrors total harmonious aliveness beyond restriction, structure or boundaries.

My breath is slow and deep, my body relaxed, my mind in a mode of sensing without judgment or explanation. I feel totally nourished, totally at one with the surroundings. I am the tree. I am the leaf. I am the fly and the squirrel. I am the water, clear and sparkling, pooled and seeping and rushing all at the same time. Which is more real? My visiting this place or the place itself? I am aware and intrinsically connected to the intricacies of the essence of evolution presented here. Connected to this *Beingness* of nature, I sense the insignificance of doing and the triviality of the atrocities man has created.

Does any spruce tree look out and see a fir as shorter? Where do we get the notion that anyone or any thing is better or worse than we are? Is the standing tree more than the whitened log lying horizontally? Or the ones that are decaying? Does it make any difference to flowers or water if I notice them? Or even that

I am here appreciating them? The water bubbles and gurgles without my admiration. Am I the only thing in the valley that sees? That cares? Am I the only one who moves in and out of awareness? My footsteps have intruded on this place. How have I altered the area by my presence? Others before and after me may follow the path that winds up the mountain. In the duality of this planet, nature exemplifies a state of Being, man magnifies a state of doing.

Nature is such an example to us. "Consider the lilies of the field how they grow."[23] Here seeds fell on nourishing ground, producing healthy plants. From the stance of their *Being*, their *doing* flowers form seeds to reproduce their kind. Giving and receiving processes abound between the plant and animal kingdoms, exemplified by the balance of water, young healthy plants, older plants near the end of their life cycles. Silhouettes of trees beyond their prime standing tall with holes where birds nest; fallen logs with chipmunk homes—giving, receiving, supporting and sustaining. We are Creation moving in the Essence of our *Being*, merged and individual, each maturing from the spark of genius pooled within our genes. None of us can totally be the other and yet all is the connectedness of evolution. This is a different space, an experience of a deeper Essence of Creation, unhurried, without necessities—an *Isness* of everything in this moment. The immortal patterning continually re-creates itself. My walk up the glacial creek has been so nourishing. I place my face in the cold, wonderful, refreshing water. An invigorating afternoon.

I wonder about numerous possibilities. I'm in awe of Creation and evolution. Off the mountain I move along a ribbon of asphalt, with my main attention set on safety while noticing the greenery encased by majestic mountains. The beauty of a large hawk surprises me as it flies from my right, coming close to the car. It suddenly banks its flight showing its underside only inches from the windshield as it continues across the roadway. I honor the magnificence of this bird and I am grateful for its quick maneuvering into another space. How free it is to be open to possibilities that bring surprises and varied experiences.

Nature is a friend, nature is a teacher. In her space is every example of human life. Your hearts open to the love shared between mother and pups, whether these be the family pet or jungle lion. You marvel at towering trees and tiny blossoms, the antics of seals and dolphins playing. You rail against civilizations' disregard of nature's example of balance and shudder at the ravages of weather. Let not your judgments discolor the beauty of experiencing the co-existence mirrored by the non-human populations of the planet. You are part of this unfolding mystery that began billions of years ago with the birth of Earth, observing and interacting with this emerging celestial body. Live your passion and learn from what you witness, always aware of your connection to planetary evolution.

Consciousness as first established on Earth was a unique energy seed, planted with the knowing that it would be a primary element in the evolution of Souls. This seed has been free to grow, become healthy, evolve. Feel the divinity in all aspects of this growth, accepting the distortions as part of the whole, not separate. As original species have cross-pollinated to create new hybrids, so has consciousness evolved, exploring every available avenue to its fullest. After all explorations and experiments have transmuted, the new emerges. Recognize *all* things as stemming from the origins of Creation's hologram. ⊛

When I was a child, my aunt, a botanist for an established seed producer, worked with hybridization, developing new varieties of flowers. She sent us packets of seeds; petunias seemed her focus. Even from the label, we didn't know just what would grow —the mystery awaited the blossoms. Our garden was embellished with double petunias, then new colors, and another summer we had ruffled ones. We kept seeds to sow the following spring creating even more mystery in their next production. We never knew what type or color would bloom.

How would we like our garden to be? What mystery are we continually planting? We prepare the soil without pushing transformative experiences—we cannot force divine energies. Life is about how we sow our seeds—fruitlessly into someone's hip pocket, into lovingly prepared soil or a pile of rocks. In self-nourishing, weeds and obstacles can be removed from the scene—old habits, thoughts, misassembled patterns. Some may be stepped on by guilt, like a barrier on top of sown seeds, blocking life forces. Forgiveness is as snow over seeds, insulating and massaging loamy dirt, supporting germination, caressing it into the cradle for new growth. We continually sow ideas without awareness, without responsibility for what happens. Awakening is like a seed sown in fertile ground by external forces for the internal Essence to grow. Disappointments can never happen when one is in the moment. Nothing can be missed or lost, because everything is present. Impatience robs one of the moment and the emerging energy.

Inspiration comes from various sources adding to the individual composite. Without one another no one would reach their potential. Each accomplishes their generic destiny, transforming into matter that furthers growth of all. Some may find themselves in the garden of another strong plant, growing with this character's support or nourishment or assistance. With any gardener's transition, other leaders arise to incorporate who they are, producing a composite, a hybrid. Every aspect is the evolution of not just that lineage; it is the evolution of All That

Is, the continual movement of discovery and expansion.

Creation is everywhere, within all aspects of the energetic disbursement. Honor all things with their individuality and in the scope of entirety. Be free within your own space, your own creation, while supporting every other aspect of this great endeavor of Creation.

Recognize all these presentations from the space of Divine Love. Each is the seed, the tender sprout, the full-grown being, portraying God in its unique way—natural Goodness being expressed intrinsically in this moment. Enlightenment honors diversity and recognizes individual peaks and valleys while supporting the flowing mystery of growing, evolving, and being life. ✱

# 22 *Personal Energy Stream Interactions*

BEING EXPOSED TO VARIOUS IDEOLOGIES and teachers stimulates personal perceptions—new concepts, emotions, and feelings. At times these may support our own logic and experience, arousing our curiosity for growth, or they may be immaterial to us at that time. This does not mean the ideas are wrong or that we lack something because we do not 'get' whatever is being shared. At that time our energy may be in a different stream, experiencing another sector of life and growth. Maybe we will interact again; maybe never. When we are unattached to this way or that way, our Soul's energy stream dictates the flow.

It has been interesting to look at the many seminars, gatherings or books that I have not been drawn to. I know that each has its place, however not for me at that time. Other people had phenomenal experiences; I was guided another way. When we have 'gut feeling' directional pulls, it is important to honor self and go with the inner guidance. However, be conscious of times when we feel drawn to opportunities and part of us digs in its heels in avoidance. Let's act from the place of conscious choice.

How do we tell which way to go or what to do for our highest good? One of my insights has been how I recognize compatibility with any physical interaction prior to or while being present with another person or group. One day I received the following message.

Presently you are connected into the energy that is circulating in resonance with the group of your friends who are meeting in Colorado. Since there is no time or distance, you are there by intention just as if you were sitting in that room. It is only personality that creates exclusion. When one moves into higher realms, they are transgressing the inner space of themselves. In personal interpretation, events appear differently although there is no difference. There is no separation; you can be anywhere another goes while concurrently being on your own path. Your energy stream is your contact with numerous 'other' realities. Intend to be present and you are. ✸

During a silent group meditation, I connected to my personal energy stream. I became aware of traveling to the leader's stream and experienced being a portion of his field. At first I was reluctant to move in, comfortable being next to it, feeling the energy. There was a presence of safety and acceptance. I realized a moment of questioning about further involvement. "If I go further, will I be engulfed? Am I wanted?" Then movement began with the message that I could hold my own while being in his stream. An ecstatic, gentle power of love was noticeable. I opened to it; it opened to me and merging began with tremendous movement. I continually grounded and opened my heart. Joy and delight expanded beyond old patterns into bliss. Physical movements began. My aura shook. I kept my breathing fairly normal while the experience continued to build, willing to experience the newness in the silent joy of bliss.

Entering a place beyond giving and receiving—a place so integrated there was no delineation between the two—it was impossible to give without receiving. There were no attachments or directions. Love was expanding. I was blessed with this experience—connection beyond any person, any group. Connection into the Allness of One. Hours later my own field still vibrated with Presence connection. My mind accepted this reality as possible. I felt blessed with co-creation. In moving free of the old, we have to let go of any identity and embrace this moment in total willingness. In being unattached, Essence creates *Now* from a new place with new energy and expansion. Imagination is the springboard, building the energy and letting go. If I touch into contraction, the moment of expansion is gone and that window closes.

From its inception everything has a connection to Source as a distinct creation composed of an individual energetic vibrational stream. We experience this as a current of energy connecting us to Creation itself. Within this stream is every lifetime on any plane and every reality of our Soul. Here our consciousness is similar to a barometer in that there is more to us than the person we see in the mirror. We can accept these numerous aspects of ourselves, initiating faster frequencies of our own GodSelf .

Life presents us with opportunities to play in one another's arenas to assist with similar lessons. When we meet someone with a kindred stream, we are attracted to that person's vibration. Relationships involve a gathering of streams to experience the magnetic forces that fuel one another in growth. A force is created when any two or more are gathered together, magnetizing a group Soul—a star-like connection point of the personal streams that holds convergent adventures to be explored. This occurs in any interaction with another person, enhancing opportunities for growth with collective lessons for individuals and the group. It is advantageous to freely experience this particular interaction and let go.

If an individual is out of personal truth her/his energy distorts and disconnects, leaving a gap in the group SoulStar. When one or more of the group feels s/he needs another to be complete or when one is out of personal integrity there is frequently a clouding of the energy. The group energy appears as clear opalescent crystal when the personal energy streams of members are connected to personal Source. Divine Plan then moves freely through each participant for manifestation. With intention the group Soul can be used as a rocket booster to propel awareness of personal empowerment. As these fire-bursts of energy complete their cycle group participants frequently find their attention attracted to other streams of energy. This movement between individuals, relationships, groups and ideologies results in the evolution of humanity. Masters, Angels, Guides all support such endeavors to experience life fully by helping us when we ask.

Within the context of every encounter are opportunities for your evolutionary development. You give names to various types of encounters, classify them as this or that to satisfy the bent to categorize in divided identifications. Keep your focus on the Oneness of this evolution, letting go of the need to understand every scrap of your experience. In the unfolding of personal awareness you use classification to identify various relationships. One such is the reference to a *twin flame*. This connection relates to someone whose lesson vibrations match your present one, presenting those little fire-bursts that mirror growth experiences for each of you.

Streams of origination create Soul streams in close vibration, a close match of energy, the term you describe as *soul mate*. There can be several streams that seem to overlap incarnating during the same time frame. This vibrational matching mirrors all aspects of the individual creation without regard to age or gender, race or location. Actual interaction may or may not occur. It depends on the paths chosen, for every encounter is perfection of the moment regardless of one's personality development.

Physical separation of distance or time has no effect on your streams. Ones that are similar are always there regardless of physical proximity. Biological families are rarely soul streams. With intention, you can connect to your soul families. Ask for this relationship to be opened to you and if they are in body at this time, the opportunity to meet can materialize. These energies are always available in spirit. The first time you choose to connect, ask someone you trust—physical or angelic—to guide your meditation through love, requesting communication with your Soul family. Welcome them as assistants on your path to self-realization.

Many people concentrate enormous amounts of energy searching for these connections. Use conscientious intention to *Be*, while accepting yourselves just as you are. This takes your awareness into stream energy for soaring into all possible adventures. Exercises to connect to HigherSelf, your Monad or God are all avenues to move consciousness into your personal stream to God. However, many teachers use their own streams by inviting participants into the leader's stream to access these faster frequencies. While it is helpful to use the stream of another for support, it is when you learn to travel in your stream that you become empowered. The level of individual connective experiences one is having is the important factor in any association with faster vibrations.

If you choose to have facilitators assist, maintain the intention to be in your own stream, detaching from others as you become aware of yours. Guru-ship involves a group held in the stream of a leader's influence. This can be productive only for a short while as a path for guidance into personal GodHood. Beyond the intention of individual growth through experiences, any holding on these levels can be detrimental. Learn, experience and *Be* from your own self. All else will be attracted to you. ❂

Words often seem confusing and are only a suggestion, an attempt to describe potent experiential energies. Just remember, there are many components to the energetic ping-pong game of life, bouncing here and there, matching for a time and moving into the next set of players. And there is the stream that is ever powerful, ever steady—*the way of Source*. We do our own work, supported by whomever we choose in the moment, with clear intention to travel in our own stream of Divinity—not to be engulfed in theirs. Personal experience of your own stream can be quite powerful, giving you a sense of connected independence to support your endeavors with less need for outside validation. As awareness expands one discovers the faster vibrations of the synthesis of all streams converging in the Void of Creation. As one participant described, "My Soul family accompanied me on a journey where I saw my thoughts, watched them leave my mind and travel into the void and create."

> *"God turns you from one feeling to another*
> *and teaches by means of opposites*
> *so that you have two wings to fly; not one."*
> Rumi

# 23 Meditation to Activate Personal Energy Stream

THE FOLLOWING MEDITATION can lead you into a personal experience of your energy stream to sense Essence connection more powerfully and open your perception to experience the energy of *Beings* heretofore unknown consciously. Notice all sensations—colors, sounds, visuals and feelings. They may have information for you. Express gratitude for their being with you and set your intention to listen.

Your Soul Family is waiting your acknowledgment. Repeating the meditation can enhance perception of these energies. My first experience with this remains quite vivid—the surprise, the joy, the excitement and the tears of gratitude. Choose your time and a space that provides at least thirty minutes of uninterrupted time for this interaction with expanded aspects of Self.

Sit comfortably in your particular safe space.

Breathe deeply, rhythmically, relaxing your body. ✸

Take your attention to your heart area, without wanting to change anything, allowing everything to be as it is. ✸

Now notice your feet connected to Earth in a place that is comfortable for you. Choose someplace that feels safe, where you are supported by nature. ✿

Set your intention to connect to your Soul at the fastest frequency possible in this moment. ✿

Breathe these energies together in the heart, inviting your heart to expand. ✿

Using breath, fill the physical body, letting the energy seep through the pores of the skin into the energetic field around your body. ✿

Extend these energies into Earth, noticing how they are received. ✿

Notice the level of safety you are experiencing. ✿

If you need to increase safety, connect even stronger to your EarthStar.

Ask particular Angelic Presences, Masters, or Beings to support you on this journey. ✿✿

Now begin to open the top of your head and breathe Soul into the pineal gland. ✿

When filled, create a channel to the hypothalamus. ✿

Breathe Soul into the hypothalamus. ✿

Extend this through the throat to fill the thymus gland ✿

Expand this spiral into your heart. ✿✿

Ask your HigherSelf to help as you ascend the bodies of your Aura. ✿

Using the breath, expand from your heart through the SoulStar,

And beyond. ✸

Set your intention to move into the fastest source vibration available to you at this time. ✸

Give yourself the freedom to expand into greater awareness of your Essence, ✸

And into your own personal spiral of Source energy. ✸

Experience this fully—all sensations, messages, visuals. ✸

Welcome your Soul Family. ✸✸✸

Be present with all they show and tell you.
(Allow several minutes for this journey.)

Gradually bring all you have experienced to your auric field. ✸

Feel the expansion of your aura as it welcomes this Soul-Family connection. ✸✸

Feel the activation as it filters into your body, ✸

Into and out of every cell at the molecular level. ✸✸

And through your body into the EarthStar, ✸

And into the core of Earth. ✸

Bring your awareness to your heart. ✸

Check your alignment with Source. ✸

Express gratitude to all who have assisted with this exercise. ✸

Set your intention to remember all messages and thoughts concerning this relationship. ✸

Take a couple of really deep breaths, open your eyes and stretch your body. ❀

Thank yourself for this experience. ❀

Stay in this open space as long as you choose, even within the activity of other events. ❧

# 24 The Black Velvet Void

As a child I frequently dreamed of a slowly rotating funnel that seemed to go down and down. Usually I was at the rim looking into this moving aberration noticing how the yellow-golden light seemed to disappear into total darkness. I recall falling into this space, awakening myself with screams. However this did not complete the episodes; sometimes I was watching, sometimes falling. These dreams continued spasmodically into early adulthood.

A fellow teacher once said that, to her, the void seemed like a black hole in space. This triggered my memory of the funnel and one day during meditation I was taken again to this place. I felt supported and safe in my surroundings so this time I chose to explore to the fullest extent available. I slid into the funnel, spiraling to the narrow, seemingly endless space of darkness that wasn't an end at all. This was not totally comfortable. Various emotions were being triggered. I sensed numerous possibilities and stayed somewhat centered as I fell.

Eventually I burst out into a space that felt so wonderful, powerful and full. There was nothing to fear, nothing to see or hear. I sensed absolute stillness, realizing no color, no feeling, no movement; nothing considered good or bad, light or dark—only space without definition. Complete silence, total nothingness and fullness. Without limits. So comfortable, like being wrapped in the silkiest of materials without weight. Such sensuousness—exquisite rapturous ecstasy. I *know* this is the Void of Creation.

Then I noticed a dot, a tiny point. The density of something incomprehensible made it distinguishable in space. My attention took me to and into the dot that exploded into Creation—from nothing into everything. As these bursts of energy expelled outward, another sphere of void was present and another spot of energy appeared. This happened over and over and over.

I realized a connection to an earlier expression where I watched the creation of sphere after sphere in the formation of everything. During the first experience I saw the bigger picture; this time I experienced the Creation's inner workings. I felt rocked, encased and embodied in the bosom of the Lord—in the void of Creation, in energies of Creation. The feelings were exquisite. Tears of gratitude flowed. Colors were intense—a sense of the evolution of color into hues that were indistinguishable until now. Loving, vulnerable, and willing; acceptance beyond description. Awesome Creation, sacredness of everything, of the physical body—its entire fields and experiences. I had a sense of the challenge and beauty of being human—of our living multi-dimensional Self.

You are here with us. We are installing a new template. Continue to bring this in. It is placing you in a more vast vibration. Use your breath to take this Light into your lungs. More oxygen into your blood stream, for Light in the blood stream nourishes the entire body through the heart. Move into the void of your physical structure. Feel the filling of your cellular structure and expand your *Being* into Earth, inviting Earth energies to celebrate with you, anchoring this template surely. A special healing of Earth comes in when this Light is activated into water bodies of the planet. This you do by channeling Light through your physical systems, mixing an air/water combination to share with Earth, feeding nature and Earth inhabitants. ✸

The filling continued for several hours; I stayed connected until I felt the expansion into Earth through my feet. They seem buried in Earth; trickles of energy moved through my legs and soles connecting to the moisture that was sucking it in, actually changing the color of the surrounding soil. I watched as it seeped into rivulets of sparkling water, gaining momentum; everything it touched was similarly changed. The streams continued to branch into all Earth's aquifer until all water was cleansed and sparkling. I watched excitedly as all planetary objects were infused with this enhanced water—as if a new chemical reaction was taking place to heal the planet. I realized whatever absorbed any of this water began a journey of alignment.

This alive experience of the void was so energizing—Creation energy. Fine prickles burst and flowed in me, filling every space, touching every cell of my body. All senses were heightened. I saw sparkles in my blood stream; I felt the swelling of the alveoli of my lungs; I could taste the sweetness of my breath.

Later I felt giddy when contemplating that space from a coherent, everyday space. I actually moved into a new experience of *being* this feeling in my life setting, without meditative practice to arrive in the void.

In void, we move into nothingness, into non-being, beyond all identification, thought and feeling. We move into lack of consciousness of anything and every thing at the same time. We let go of knowing, feeling and being—a place beyond memory. We come back knowing we have experienced depths of God as this Energy manifests to us in this moment. Meditation into nothingness is the world of illusion dissolving into freedom where 'I' does not exist; where there is no awareness of 'I.' Therefore there is no search, no effort, no thing to give or receive.

I have had numerous personal experiences of this space, each slightly different from any other. Description is beyond any definition. Clients who have chosen to look into their own places of total darkness have moved beyond the place where fear had prevailed. With encouragement and assistance all have challenged themselves to bravely explore the dark. All have come into Oneness with the Void, allowing fear to be transformed into the excitement of greater possibilities. Perceptions alter. Lives change as we consent to look at every sensation, emotion, thought and encounter straight on rather than deflecting them. Food tastes better; hearing is sharpened; colors have a heightened intensity; perceptual vision expands. The significance of our relationships intensifies to include all aspects with awareness that loving ourselves is as important as loving them. I accept that who others are is who I am. We are our own masters, healers and guides to the internal and eternal love and joy emerging as compassion for ourselves. In completing each moment we actualize these unified spaces enhancing all life.

For each of us, exploring the void has not been something we decided ahead of time to do. As our fields are cleared of disempowering energies, directives seem to come from our Soul as to presenting the time frame for these powerful experiences and the resulting transmissions. I am aware that my personal experience has opened the channel to support others in the appropriate setting and time for their own journey into the void. Perhaps this exposure will instigate your curiosity to the extent that you will be supported in such an experience. I urge you to be in a safe place with someone who is willing to support you with compassion and willingness to stay present no matter what happens. For any empowering endeavor I strongly suggest you take your intention into meditation, connecting to your HigherSelf, Soul and Monad and ask for their guidance. Their assistance is valuable; their acceptance is complete Love.

# 25 Life Ascending

WE ARE EACH where we are for whatever reason, frequently beyond mental understanding. Until the active elements are fully experienced, there might be no room for another perspective. I've learned, at least for me, when I notice my emotions or thoughts are taking control, it's time to stop, relax and be present in another way. I can sit with discomfort—mine or yours—without 'doing' to hide it or change it or fix it. This space honors the present moment with all the stuff. However, there are still times I feel uncomfortable, such as watching others treat themselves in unloving ways, or 'damning' their actions or attempting to 'kill' their own enthusiasm, eat too much, failing to recognize the beauty of everyday life. I am learning to let go of needing them to be any other way, to accept our combined present realities.

What does it take to be compassionate rather than judging? Judgments entangle me in their circumstances; compassion reflects their Soul. I recall a quote purportedly from Socrates about the pain of enlightenment being little in relation to the pain of noticing another person's potential not being lived fully. Sensing discomfort is part of life. If I am triggered by the reactions of others it is about me—not them. *Everything* in life is really a mirror, whether we like it or not. I show you to you; you show me to me. I recall asking a teacher why some people felt I pushed their buttons. His reply was for me to consider that one of the demonstrations of being on the path of enlightenment is mirroring the personal perspective of another—without being entangled in any outcome.

There is an old Zen story of the teenager who became pregnant. She was terrified to admit who the father was, so when pressed for details, she named a monk in the monastery. The village was outraged to think the monk would do something like this. They waited until the baby was born before they climbed the steep hill to the monastery. When the monk came to the gate, they handed the infant to him saying, "This is your child. You must keep it." His only reply was, "Ah so," as he took the child.

Nine years later when the young mother was dying, she confessed that the father was really the butcher's son. The villagers were outraged at themselves about their earlier decision. They hurriedly climbed to the monastery to tell the monk of their mistake, saying they were so sorry and would take this burden from him. He graciously listened and said, "Ah so," as he gave the boy to the villagers.

Realize there is a major question being asked, questioning one's authentic nature of Godness. Doubt is an energy penetration attempting to discredit the integrity of you who walk in Light. The perception of your own true nature, the 'YourSelf,' is the key to withstanding these onslaughts. Many succumb to the easy way out, retreating as a turtle, peeking out now and then to check the atmosphere. Many of you have been these mortals in shells for lifetimes. You have gone your way, the most comfortable way, the easy way with the flow of humanity. Others become staunch bulls, knowing they are physically all-powerful while pushing their way into the scattering crowds. There is another way to channel this power. Stand in your Light. Recognize the effects of these energies on the masses and attend to your own emotions, your feelings and thoughts about what is happening. Turtles and bulls do have a heart. Know YourSelf and interact fully in life. ✷

It is important for you to recognize who you are, your present ability and potentiality. Even the name you call yourself is Essence encoded. To activate this, use the following exercise, setting aside at least fifteen minutes of personal time, away from all duties.

৵

Sit comfortably in a private place.

Say the name you are known by in as many ways, tones, frequencies as you can.

State it forcefully and gently.

Whisper it, say it loudly.

Sound it out phonetically, spell it letter by letter, forward and backward.

Continually be aware of feelings that surface.

Is there any tension, restriction?

Does a particular pronunciation or resonance make you want to stop speaking?

What does this name really mean to you?

Notice how it connects to generational history.

Pay attention to whatever messages, voices or feelings surface as you continue to verbally share this vibration. Mentally note them and move on with continuous repetitions for at least five minutes.

Stay very connected to yourself and these vibrations as you come into silence.

Really feel your body, particularly your mouth and throat.

Notice what you want to 'spit' out; what you want to take in.

Connect to your heart, becoming aware of its palpitations. Is there expansion or contraction?

Invite your HigherSelf to answer any questions that arise.

For any contraction, ask to be shown how to assist this aspect in its evolution.

Be with all feelings, knowing within you are all answers.

Ask the Love Presence in your heart to expand to include all of you, including your name.

Sense the freedom in being you.

And when you are ready, bring your consciousness to your entire physical body, sitting as you are, in this moment.

Be fully conscious of your surroundings and all that has just transpired, knowing additional information will be available as needed.

Thank yourself for this experience. ❧

When you stay in touch with who you are beyond the mind, you will weather energetic battles without scars. Remember every one is in the life of YourSelf and all others, *to support your awareness of the truth that God Is every moment.* Verbally express your truth to those who support you. Utilize awareness that the comfortable 'old way' is only energy moving through the atmosphere, attempting to hook you into remaining within that edifice. Many will fall into the trap temporarily. Strength continually builds confidence to support your stating feelings truthfully and accepting your being Light. What you accept, others in your company can learn to accept.

Continue connecting into your origins. Be with people because of their connection to similar energies. Stay in your heart with all of this, accepting Self as neutral; no need to engage the mind. This does not label you different. You are Oneness; keep your awareness on One. And watch the differentiation. Feel us—we are always here.

Does considering, recognizing and expressing our unfolding truths change our daily lives?

The act of expressing your feelings demands change —just by the energetics of verbal expression. It is important to share in the moment from the heart with those who are part of the experience. Remember they are a reflection—not the cause. Then fully explore the energy with intention to complete the cycle. As it passes through your fields it will gather idle energies. If you choose to hold onto these energies your experience of them is intensified. Relax; surrender to the expression so there are no hooks, no sticky places for these adverse energies to cling. Where there is no tension the movement continues the journey cleanly, taking its entire kin with it. This is transformation—opening yourself to discordant activities while being willing for conflicting energies to pass through your field. In this process related particles are cleansed as well—the action of healing with Light.

You witness those who hold onto unproductive energies, complicating their lives, creating an even stronger expression of the invading action—an invitation for disruptive energies. This adventure is to love everyone whatever they are in any moment and with compassion, support them in understanding another way of behavior. We all made this decision together. There are supporters on the planet at this time with unperceived compassion, choosing various modes of delivery to discover which one works best to ignite a deeper love within the general populace. This is why many of you have changed your interactions, using different styles to encourage others to uncover that space within themselves. This impacts many levels of existence. The activity here will expand and blend into the activity there and there until peace is accomplished. It is not hopeless until it doesn't work. Perseverance and patience is required, continually embodying more of your GodHood.

Realize the pertinent job right now is to expand your ability for compassion. Understand that this support shared unobtrusively and directly, assists others in opening their hearts further. Light continues to shine even when something shadows Its beam. There is nothing that can totally obscure It; the beam is much broader than any encumbrance. It is like a stream of water that continually flows onto a rock, gradually, gently eroding the surface tension to expose what lies underneath. And in the process, indentations may be formed where another life-form can manifest for its season of life. All part of Divinity in action.

Think of how you can use this concept; bring in Light, hold it; bring in more, hold it, creating a greater and greater expression of Light. With any expression you either hold onto the energies or let them pass into Light. When you have no similar energies to hook these aggressors, they move so swiftly that you fail to notice. You are participating in ascension, in Universal transformation.

One of the things that happens with the choice to accept

Light is that you become conduits for the ascension of everything. In this space one agrees to open his/her fields to all energies, regardless of origin, including the willingness to experience every one of them if necessary for transformation. This does not mean that you experience them to the degree they act in your world. In other words, just because you experience rage to the point of murder, you do not have to commit the act. You become conduits to transmute this energy. Each of you has the capability to be a healing conductor. When you commit to fully accepting Divinity, you open YourSelves to the holographic knowledge that you accept healing responsibilities—embodiment of Divinity in the perfection of every moment. Be aware of your intentions and express all feelings in the moment without attachment—a big key.

You can work with, beside, or go hand in hand with someone and still carry your uniqueness. Even your own hand has its representations in the way it perceives what it touches, its signature imprint. You can add no more fingers. And you learn to use the whole synchronously with each part playing its unique role. So it is when you work closely with another, whether in a job situation, a friendship, an art project, community activities or planetary ascension. The absence of anyone who is committed to the journey creates a hole that must be filled by someone else. It is when one feels a necessity to engage in more than their unique part of the whole that perplexity arises, like one member choosing to be the thumb while it is already another finger. Such projection relates to not feeling understood or affirmed, mirroring discomfort for that ego's actuality.

When you touch something with your middle finger, four others react to that touch, even though they were not physically involved. So it is with groups holding the same focus. Acknowledge the unique manifestations of the moment while letting go of needing them to look any particular way. Be relaxed with all results, knowing even though their necessity was not previously foreseen, now they are vital for the end result—even when this creates another version of the original plan. Evolution in process. Totally unpredictable. Love flows as the stream infiltrating all reflections with no direction or boundaries.

Compassion for others involves being unattached to what anyone does or doesn't do. As you learn to balance and integrate, your own conscious caring develops into deep generosity without attachment to anyone doing anything other than what they are doing. Develop the capacity to hold love to such a degree that you are willing to stand back while others exert their energies even when you see diverse options available. Hear the clear message about detachment as a powerful route into heart action. Follow any inner call for revised responses rather than pursue previous plans. The preferred focus is expansion into Wholeness. Here you hold unlimited possibility for others as a response from your unique design as a sovereign aspect of God. ❀

I look at the responsibility that any of us *could* feel and realize it is just one more thing for unwanted energies to hook into. All of this concerns that phrase we avoid hearing—"Let Go. Surrender!" Let go of old beliefs in order to contain the energy of manifestation; enlarge the realms of possibility. Create space for expansion, breathe, receive and let go. Give and open to receiving while holding only to the movement of ascension. Acknowledge Now and *let go!*

꩜ I am in a space of awe, of extension, of wanting to *Be* without doing, while at the same time I am aware of moving my *Beingness* into 'doing'—activity for the body while the expansiveness of me is devouring and integrating information presented. The free flowing-ness feels so connected to what I *know* within, so connected to Spirit. I accept I am only touching the hem of the concept's magnitude. I ask for my human composite to expand into *Beingness*, into the probability of my mind working for my DivineSelf rather than the opposite. I am suddenly aware of a longing for woods to walk in—or an ocean to sit beside or be in. It is a lesson in accepting my *Beingness* in whatever situation or location I am and surrendering to a new experience of MySelf. ❧

I recall a walk along the edge of a large meadow. The scolding sounds of birds attracted my attention. Standing very still I noticed two wrens hopping up and down a limb, their tails lifted in alarm. As they continued others flew into this tree until there were at least a dozen warning the forest of my intrusion. I recalled my mother reading to us T*he Burgess Bird Book for Children,*[24] a wonderful dialogue from Jenny Wren about interaction between birds and animals in their habitat, quite a teaching about relationships.

Here was the largest congregation of wrens I had ever observed. I stood still, trespassing no further. There seemed to be no other animals around and yet they joined together fiercely protecting their habitat in nature's instinctual manner, continuing until I was quite a distance from that tree. I am used to a form of this scenario where usually a bird warns of any human's invasion into the world of nature. However, this banding together was a new version. In late July they were not protecting nests. Something beyond my comprehension was happening.

Months later I saw a correlation. My heart palpitated, tears formed. I remembered to breathe deeply. Truth was being presented. The fact was the wrens felt some type of threat. I knew I was no threat to them, however something within them found this something new in their normal world discomforting. I could not understand their attitude. They were not willing to stop their actions, to return to their pattern of life until I moved out of their range. Interactions with people frequently threaten some unperceived aspect of us causing indefinable reactions, be these positive or negative. We share and seem to be rejected because the other has no reference to our reality. And others welcome interaction. It is up to us to decide our willingness to continue the exchange —as a casual acquaintance, friend or peer. If fear is activated, we can defend ourselves by moving the other way quickly or by creating an atmosphere for an angry exchange. I can give what I have; I can receive in relation to what I accept that I have. All interchanges are in relation to this concept of exchange, right down to our earning money to pay for goods and services. If the grocer doesn't have what we want, we have to look elsewhere. If our customers don't want certain goods, we discontinue the stock.

So it is in our lives. There are things we want, ideas that intrigue us. We find a source that is supposed to have the answers; maybe it does. Or discomfort arises and we continue the search to live in our authenticity—frequently without any understanding from those involved. We communicate as we *Be*—loving, skeptical, compassionate, concerned, advising—all from the projection of the active parts of ourselves that are creating this moment. Whatever the response, it is perfect for accessing the experience. Living in fear acts like a magnet to other apprehensive people just as being compassionate attracts loving interactions.

Everyone is comfortable in his or her chosen surroundings until personality detects discomfort and supports moving into a different setting. So it is with any interchange involving mind and emotions disconnected from HeartSelf. Be open to possibilities, where anything can emerge. My direction is not your direction. Your optimum experience is based on all your experiences, mine on mine. Every one of us is geared to unique expressions, even in circumstances that seem the same. Who am I to tell you what to do? To ask you to change your behavior? My commitment is to myself, living from my heart to know us and God. And in our joint adventure we are continually evolving—evolution living a life of ascension.

# 26 Meditation to Integrate Relationships

THIS PARTICULAR MEDITATION is designed to connect and clear energies between two people—in whatever kind of relationship exists. It is powerful with both people present, however, it can be used *in absentia* by inviting the Spirit of the person to participate. It is very important to let this Spirit energy know you are coming from love without any expectations of their assistance. Connect to your HigherSelf and then ask their HigherSelf if it is appropriate for you to interact at this time. If you do not have a convincing "yes," this is not the time to be with them. This is for your own personal development. *It is not about an other person*. Each person involved receives just what is available for him or her in those moments.

You need to be experienced with HigherSelf connection. See Chapter 4 for this meditation. HigherSelf connection needs to be clear and strong prior to working with anyone—particularly *in absentia*.

This particular meditation will be more powerful if you create a tape in your own voice. Leave blank tape-time for your process. Set your intention to turn the tape off and on if you feel rushed.

ભ

Sit comfortably and relax in your particular special space.

Breathe deeply, relaxing your body. ❋

Take your attention to your heart area, without wanting to change anything, allowing everything to be as it is. ❋

Now notice your feet connected to Earth in a place that is comfortable. ❋

Set your intention to connect to your Soul at the fastest frequency possible in this moment. ❋

Invite the heart to expand as you move into this stream of personal empowerment. ❋

Bring these energies together in the heart and fill the physical body, letting the stream seep through the pores of the skin into the energetic field around your body. ❋ ❋

Extend this stream into and through your EarthStar, being aware of the reception by EarthBeings. ❋

Feel this connection—Heart, Soul and Earth. ❋

Invite your personal Guardians and Angels to be present. ❋

Ask your HigherSelf to guide every aspect of this meditation. ❋

Be aware of your HigherSelf signal. ❋

If you are unclear, ask your HigherSelf to intensify the signal. ❋

Now take your awareness to the energy of the person you're choosing to work with. ❋

Ask the other person's HigherSelf if it is appropriate to have this interaction at this time. ⊛

If you sense any reluctance, thank their HigherSelf for the recognition and bring your energy back to yourself. Acknowledge that this is an inappropriate time for whatever reason. *Do not force any interaction.*

Only when you have a clear signal to proceed: ⊛

Thank their HigherSelf for being open to assist you with your own healing. ⊛

Re-acknowledge your personal energy stream. ⊛

Ask the other person's HigherSelf to assist your intention to feel their energy stream. ⊛

Recognize any similarities and differences in the way your two streams feel. ⊛

Explore their stream, paying attention to all sensations and visuals that might appear. ⊛ ⊛

Take your awareness to the place where your streams meet, noticing the point of convergence, your group SoulStar. ⊛ ⊛

Ask this energy body for any messages) that are appropriate at this time. ⊛ ⊛

Return your awareness to your own heart area; notice its feelings. ⊛ ⊛

Notice any changes. ⊛ ⊛

Now extend your heart energy to your partner, being fully aware of every feeling. ⊛ ⊛ ⊛

Come back into your own stream. Notice your heart. ⊛

Notice your grounding. ⊛

Be aware of your personal Soul-energy stream. ✸

Set your intention to strengthen this integrative connection. ✸

Now extend your first chakra energy—the body's pelvic floor, to your partner. ✸

Be aware of safety feelings. ✸

Be aware of trust, of how you are or are not feeling secure in this relationship. ✸ ✸

Come back into your own stream. Notice your heart, your grounding, your personal energy stream. ✸ ✸

Set your intention to strengthen your connection even more. ✸

Extend your second chakra energy—belly area—to your partner. ✸

How do your inner children relate? ✸

Is there a sense of play? ✸

Of joy? ✸

Notice the level of creativity in your relationship. ✸

Be aware of giving and receiving energy. ✸

Notice any feelings of aliveness. ✸

Notice any feelings of passion. ✸

Return to your own stream. Notice your Heart, Earth and Soul energies. ✸

Set your intention to strengthen your personal energy stream. ✸

Notice the amount of energy needed to bring yourself into balance. ✦✦

Extend your third chakra energy—waistline area—to your partner. ✦

Is there control energy being projected or received? ✦

Do you feel any need to support the other? ✦

Or to be supported by him/her? ✦

Notice all feelings, emotions and messages that surface. Stay with anything that comes up, being open for its transformation. ✦✦✦

Come back into your own stream. Notice your Heart, Earth and Soul energy stream. ✦

Extend your fifth chakra energy—throat area—to your partner. ✦

Listen for any messages. ✦

Return your attention to your Heart, Soul, Earth connection. ✦

Notice any changes—is there openness or contraction? ✦

Bring your awareness to your fourth chakra energy—heart area. ✦

Being fully aware of feelings, emotions or thoughts, extend your heart to this partner. ✦

Keep your attention on the energy you are sending as well as your partner's energy. ✦✦

Is there openness or contraction on either end? ✦

Pay attention to all HigherSelf messages. ✦

Notice your visions of this relationship. ❀

Be aware of your feelings and intentions. ❀

Bring your attention back to your own stream. ❀

Notice your Heart, Earth and Soul energy stream. ❀

How does this exercise impact your willingness to be connected to this person? ❀

Ask your HigherSelf to be even more present for you now as you move into silence. ❀

Listen for messages that your HigherSelf may have for you. ❀ ❀

Ask questions if you choose, being very receptive to answers. ❀ ❀ ❀

(If you are making a tape for this meditation, allow several minutes of quiet time for this step.)

Bring your awareness to your heart. ❀

Reconnect to the Earth. ❀

Check your alignment with Source. ❀

Express gratitude to those who have assisted with this exercise. ❀

Set your intention to remember all messages and thoughts concerning this relationship.

Take a couple of really deep breaths, open your eyes and stretch your body. ❀

Thank YourSelf for this experience. ❧

# 27 My Journey into a Manure Pile

DURING ONE very powerful meditation I am taken to the floor of the Earth, into the refuse areas of the planet—from the decay on the forest floor to a manure pile, from a pile of rotting fruit to a dead animal with maggots. Whatever I am shown, there is beauty. I am drawn to scenes of the farmyard barn where I milked cows as a teenager. I sense the barnyard chore of shoveling the cow manure out of the trough designed to catch it during the milking process, through a hole in the wall into the manure pit, into all the teeming organisms for the transformation of this material into fine grains of loamy compost. During spring cleaning this fertilizer is transferred to the garden and pasture. I recall the stench; however, now it's connected with another thought pattern. Here in this manure pile, Creation is at work. In the breakdown of this material is the beginning of life—birth. And if left alone this pile will someday flatten, becoming a hotbed for plants rather than the present nursery of insects.

In a wooded area I see the remains of an animal in a similar activity of nature, the decay evolving as the breeding ground for numerous species. Dead plants, sticks and leaves create fruitful soil and fertilizer for the forests in which spores of mold enhance the birth of decay. I see these cycles—leaves, twigs, trees, the thriving organisms in each phase of life/death—holding space for other numerous forms of earth energy in various transformational stages. Even in water—leaves that fall into streams, lakes, serving as fertilizer and food for microorganisms.

I am shown myself working on the farm of my youth, burying plant matter. Composting available scraps and cuttings freed us from the cycle of flies while feeding those miracle performers—earthworms and grubs creating soil that naturally nourishes our garden. I see the activity of preparing worms for fishermen, the process of moving material from the worm beds to a table to place 100 worms into each carton, along with enough dirt to keep them healthy. The smell of this compost is earthy, virile.

The evolution of the food chain moves all the way into our human food sources and back into defecation-and-decay energy cycles. I see rain massaging and snow insulating the loamy dirt, caressing it into a cradle for new growth. I sense the beauty of the organisms thriving in these places, transforming earth material into fertilizer that feeds every aspect of nature's growth. The engaging process of bodily death and decay nurtures all of Earth—the return of earth material to earth material, whether animal or plant. The sense of nothing wasted fills me, transforming beliefs about the refuse of natural endeavors. Everything nourishes something else—regardless of what we think. Who are we as people to assume we are chosen to be more than a fly or a worm? Creation Is!

I am shown Creation as a sphere with wavering lacy edges and a dot in its center. The dot expands itself in a spherical motion as a yolk growing until it touches the edges. With this contact the lacy edges smooth and stabilize. Division happens in a controlled explosion forming another sphere. It links into the first sphere from its edge and into the center of the next in a continual development of spheres. Within this movement each sphere rotates internally from its center to edge, back into the center as if the center continually becomes outside and the outside moves to center, cycling out and in, in and out with a pulsation of creative rhythm. The external rotation moves similarly to that of planets in orbit.

I have a clear sense of my own cells as similar spheres. In their movement they continually divide and multiply, creating other cells that repeat the pattern. I watch this growth process in color within my own arm—multidimensional development. I see an individual cell, the spiraling movement beginning slowly, undulating in its rotation until there is an eruption into two cells. Everything settles, seems momentarily still before the process is repeated. Although each component of my body has different cells, their movement and division is similar—faster or slower, depending upon energetic functions. They fill; they rotate; they repeat themselves in the creation of new cells. This movement from the center to the edge is spherical and continual—creating and recreating in its movement. Movement, birth and death is the ongoing creation of this planet.

When we embody the whole of the physical form and all its ramifications, an infusion occurs that is without separation from Earth *and* is totally being God. No one goes alone. Many people want to *Be* without embodying the whole of Earth—the garbage and the beauty. *Every thing* known and unknown in the Universe moves together in this evolution of Source. We exist, we take, we give, we cry, we laugh, we hate, we love, we live, we die. And we discover.

Coming into union, into Oneness, is beyond separation, into merging all ideas, concepts, thoughts, and expressions of separation. The human mind has quite a difficult time with this concept, similar to its grasping that there is no way to disconnect from love. You are the tree, the manure, the automobile, the water, the worms, the human. There is no difference regardless of what mind and science have discovered. In order to conceive the fullness, one encounters differences *just to experience what those elements might feel like, look like, act like, and be.* This unfoldment expresses how ideas invent illusions, inviting you to see a multitude of expressions as you realize there is no differentiation. You have taken things apart, dissected these parts and put them together again. You have reduced and expanded pieces, all in the search for God. You move along these paths until you arrive at the beginning where there is no search. It is all no thing—every thing. One. Unification. Creation.

Those of you who are returning your attention to One comprise the mass forerunners, numbers of whom have never been in one place before. Many dimensions know these concepts as truth; however, Earth explorations include the application of this knowledge. Since you are All One, there is no aloneness. Every *thing* you contact is you—not part of you. 'Parts' indicate separation. Watch your language to instill empowerment you become a clear mirror reflecting Oneness. ✸

Seeing separation propels us into searching for something that we feel we have lost, that has been taken from us. What if we imagine that there is no thing to re-connect? What if we accept being All That Is?

That you are; and also the flower of spring, the wheat at harvest, the grub in its burrow under snow. Image completeness—Wholeness of Creation. There is no where to go; nothing else to *Be* beyond what each is in this moment. In this place doing *exactly* what you are doing—be this joy or pain. You see, this is the only way one can accept the moment, the space of Creation, of God. Nothingness does away with separation for there is no thing to be separated from. Everything is so inclusive that separation is impossible. Let the mind say, "I don't know... maybe I can accept this." "If I can live this way..." Even though the mind has been trained to examine, to extract and explicate facts, to delve into cracks and crannies, it cannot separate itself either. Its agenda is not to discover something that is different or separate, new or old, but to expose All That It Is.

This awareness is the nucleus of your search. Because there are numerous ones who embody these truths, you can uncover it within your experiences. *Be* within the possibility with intention of *Being* the Divine collective, sacred Spirit in action. ❀

❧ I have enveloped and been encompassed by another transmission of energy beyond words. Tears flow; my heart sings; my physical vehicle seems to swell. Divine memory is being activated. My heart knows this distillation. I am filled with ecstasy, spiritual sensuality. The spiral moves in and upon itself with total inclusion. Awesome reality.

My intention is to continue enveloping the magnitude of combined streams in this natural entelechy of Divine Life cycles. My field continues its spiral to include the emotional and physical bodies involving every cell and atom in this evolution. It's as though I am being 'broken down,' composting the mental body's memory of One.

I am aware of a lack of any attachment to any concept or experience being God—or not being God. It is as It is. I check to see if there is any ego attempting to create some illusion by identifying God. Right *Now* I sense total love and the freedom to simply *Be*. I see spirals within spirals, undulating, rotating, toning—energies filled to capacity, moving in magnification of themselves. My heart is nourished and filled, expanding into new territory. There is a silence within, a peace that permeates in every direction. With integration of Union, I am One—I Am. I Am That. I Am that I Am.

# 28  Uncovering Enlightenment

EACH OF US is held lovingly where we are—trusting the moment is the key. *Being* enhances our lives with unusual events beyond our imagination. Let's excite our senses instead of feeling the same old thing. Let's move beyond thinking we are in control. Let's expand into something new, something exciting. And challenge ourselves to expand our connection to Spirit, adding another dimension to how and what we do. Let's reflect who we are. The path each of us is living is our path of enlightenment. The result of some event or circumstance in our lives encourages us to consider a different view of reality, opening to an up-until-now oblivious possibility. I read somewhere that the majority of enlightened people on this planet live ordinary lives in relative obscurity. Joseph Campbell shared his regrets that illumination comes too late. Blessed are those in our lives with whom the keys to enlightenment reside. Blessed are those who uncover their keys and live to be reflective guides.

In order to be truly alive, to really be vital beings, we have to be completely in this moment. I am who I am right now. It's not about who I am going to be in the next moment. It's not about what someone told me I was six months ago, two days ago. It is who I am *Now*. My mind cannot describe, cannot know who this being is. It isn't about the mind. It comes from within me, every single moment. It is about how I am experiencing me and you and existence right now. When we are into story or tales about what was or what might be or what can be or what could be we aren't totally alive. We aren't present.

Present means right here right now. In her book, *The Writing Life,* Annie Dillard shares, "Why are we reading if not in hope that the writer will magnify and dramatize our days, will illuminate and inspire us with wisdom, courage, and the possibility of meaningfulness, and will press upon our minds the deepest mysteries, so we may feel again their majesty and power?"[25]

You are reading these words because there is something here for you, to inspire you, to move you into being more of who you are. It has nothing to do with whether you do it in the manner of anyone else, none of us do things the same way. It is about saying, "Okay. Let's look at this." It is about encouraging you to blend all your resources into being you as I am blending me and resources that are available to me. In this space we evolve who we are in this moment, into who we are in this moment and who we are in this moment. Leave anything out and life doesn't work.

Our lives are continual movement, only stopped by the mind—particularly when we use it to avoid noticing pain lurking in places that feel unloved, unlived. We feel discomfort whether it is within ourselves or someone else. Pain is a cry for love, it wants love, they want love—we want love. We recognize what our mind would like *now* to be—this way or that way, its wants and desires. We move into power when we connect to 'this is the way it is.' Let's open our preferences to something totally new—outside the mind into all possibility. Live totally in the fullness of this moment—a state of continual connection to All That Is. Maybe here we connect to enlightenment.

What is enlightenment? Look at the phrase, in light. One of several definitions is when we recognize and realize that *we are Light.* It's not something we know; its meaning comes from deep within our Being. This doesn't mean that we stand on a street corner and yell, "I am Light." Enlightenment is not a mental exercise. It is cellular memory, consciously activated by internal listening. As we connect into such a depth of Light, it oozes out, manifesting in our everyday lives. Those who have their own intention to connect within feel the reflection from others who carry these energies. Recently someone attending a meditation I was leading told me she was there because previously she sat beside me in a meeting and felt the peacefulness, the quietness, and she wanted to know more about it. Another lady recently shared with me how she connected with my energy, feeling a permeating peacefulness. Her identification was internal elegance. A part of me doesn't identify with any of this, and yet I also know that the changes in my life in the past thirty years have been dramatic. I am not saying this is or represents enlightenment; I wonder if any of us knows for sure. There is a part of my mind that says, "Nah" and yet others tell me that this is what's happening. They say the portals have been opened, thus enlightenment can be a lot easier than in the past. The mental body says, "but...but...but...but," while our integrated Self comes into consciousness as the director of the new being that is opening to all possibilities and connecting to the expanse of Source for all we can contain moment to moment. What I know is that my life is easier, simpler. For instance, patience just is—most of the time. I recall one of the many messengers I have heard, sharing with me when I was appreciating his patience. He said he had no need for patience because he had no impatience.

Several years ago I realized that I was spending a lot of energy attempting to understand many things that didn't make any difference. So with my intention of letting go of things that were using my energy, I let go of the need to understand. I became unattached to it. This isn't something I did overnight, it is ongoing. And yet, there is no need to understand things. This does not say that I don't understand, it simply says that I don't *need* to. Understanding is always present. If a question is not answerable immediately, there is always someone to ask or some place to look it up. In mental attempts to search for the whys, we narrow our vision by concentrating on rational explanations as per our societal upbringing. Our focus becomes one-sided in this examination of knowledge, shutting out undefinable possibilities. This precludes our grasping extended energies that are ever present—those that finally produce a surprise, a perspective that spawns a new result. Results can be astounding when we acknowledge our peripheral vision, be it actual or imaged.

What do we want to carry with us in our sack of goodies, the identification we give ourselves? Do we need to carry this and this and this? Do we need these things with us every moment or are they tools we can pick up when the time is right? For instance, when I am driving in my car I don't necessarily need my hiking boots. And yet, if I were going hiking, I certainly would. They could be available within the car should I decide to take a hike.

In all interactions much occurs beyond the obvious. Each of us exists beyond the conscious; we are knowers of ancient wisdom that taps into everything. Any belief, choice or understanding can be confining. Keep everything open, ready for new material, new energy, letting go of definition. Although we use terms like 'levels of awareness' perhaps there are no such things —no levels, no colors, chakras, bodies, etc.—only God unfolding, or possibly not even this. Maybe nothing real can be threatened and nothing unreal exists.

Meditation brings a powerful peace that is frequently heightened when we hold a intention for emptiness and mystery. Separation dissolves, individual and communal awareness surfaces. Frequently the adventure of spiritual growth expands into some state of maturity, always flexible and expanding. When I am in meditation I have no need to define who I am or what I will be doing tomorrow. In fact perhaps I never need to know either of these. In this moment this is who I am. In this moment this is what I am doing. In this moment this is who I am.

I was probably forty years old before I heard the word 'meditation.' When I participated in the experience of what was termed meditation, it was a reconnection to childhood Quaker Meeting—listening for and to the Holy Spirit. Meditation for me is a way of life. At times meditative experiences are profound, taking varying amounts of time to integrate. Writing is one mode of integration. Meditation comes from within, activating compassion that moves from inside out—the experience of *everything* all around me. If I am everything, I choose to welcome totality within me, being present with all questions, all experiences and awarenesses. Include everything, the AllOne.

Sitting in stillness helps us see ourselves in relationship to our world, the universe, All That Is. This connection integrates our individualism with the rhythmic flow of Essence. As we choose to unconditionally be all that we can be in every moment, accepting the limitations of the mind, we make ourselves available without holding. Inspiration and expanded perceptions of possibilities surface.

After a good night's sleep, when we awaken without interruption, there is a time/space where the deep relaxation of sleep continues, a space of peaceful union with self. I recall an experience when I was the caretaker of the building we used for a school; I slept in the building. I was not needed to be part of the early morning schedule; other duties required my time. I would wake up conscious of the sounds of the morning activities and lie there in my own personal meditation in resonance with the background. I recall one morning knowing I didn't want to interrupt this place, this sensation of connectedness. This was more than a physical place; more than physical relaxation. A spiritual connection was present. A message came through very clearly. "You don't have to interrupt this. You can keep this space while in your activities." This was a surprising and intriguing message. I lay very still to absorb the possibilities. The message returned with "Do it." Setting my intention to hold the state, I carefully began to move. That first morning, it probably lasted about five minutes after I got out of bed. Since then, this state has continued to increase until most of the time I am aware of being there; however, my mind does not always hold the fact that I am. During everyday activities, when I stop to check in, I find my body has the associated sensations I get while in deep meditation. For me this represents that a lot of me stays in that space most of the time. I feel it is a matter of accepting that each of us is who we are, doing what we are doing as we continue to open ourselves to experience our spirit.

Experiences with people and events may seem separated from any state of connected presence and yet, underneath our consciousness, we can find that essence quality inherent in each of us. We spend a lot of time tied up in "what ifs" and "without this I can't..." or "this requires that I..." Maybe all of it is an opportunity for us to say, "Oh, this is interesting. This can be done this way." Or it can be done this way ... or this way... or this way. Infinite possibilities Little things, big things, all part of the whole me. No matter how they appear.

Choosing to experience beyond past occurrences alters our reactions and creates a new experience for this particular situation. Risks involve the heart, the heart of seeing ourselves. The heart knows this moment as the joy and excitement called *life*. Enlightened? Could it really be possible? Do I dare think this way?

> "Who am I? It matters not that you know who I am;
> it is of little importance.... It is what you cannot see
> that is so very important. I am one who is propelled by
> the power of faith; I bathe in the light of eternal wisdom; I am sustained by the unending energy of the
> universe; this is who I really am!"
>
> Peace Pilgrim[26]

# 29 Early Morning Meditative Experience

CONSIDER THIS a learning step toward expanding meditation into all activities. As with any new practice, repeated experiences deepen the process. This meditative practice is very powerful in my life. Have fun with your experience.

To begin this experience, choose an evening when you know you can awaken the next morning without an alarm clock or any other interruption. If you sleep with someone, tell the person that you would appreciate not being disturbed during your morning awakening, that you want to be left alone until you decide to arise.

Just before going to sleep this night, read through this and set your intention to be conscious of your state of sleep when you awake in the morning.

Ask your Guides to support you in this plan and go to sleep as usual.

With practice you will awake, realizing you are 'awake' with a sense of your body being somewhat separate from the part of you that is aware.

You know you are lying in bed, that your body seems to be asleep while in a much more relaxed space than usual, similar to deep meditation. (In deep meditation there is frequently no mental comprehension.)

You have consciousness and thoughts about this state. You are aware of body sensations and you are not directing anything.

It is as if you are watching yourself *Be*.

Consider this as a connection to Spirit, which is always present with or without your awareness.

No part of you wants to move; you are perfectly comfortable regardless of body placement.

Continue noticing all feelings, thoughts and sensations.

Notice if and when ego wants to interrupt with other things that 'must' be done.

Gently tell these voices you hear them and will pay attention later.

Be conscious of other sounds in the area without needing to do anything about them.

Continue to 'watch' yourself in this expanded state. Gratitude may surface; tears may flow. Watch and *Be*.

You might sense or hear the voice of your HigherSelf. Pay particular attention to any messages you receive from this source. Or ask a question if you choose.

In this space of *Being* you can view possible events of your day with intention to be in relationship with all activities from this present awareness state. (Don't berate yourself when you find yourself in one of these interactions with an active personality rather than this inner *Beingness*. It takes practice.)

At some point you will notice you are beginning to really wake up; the body wants to move.

Again check your physical sensations, anchoring them as an indication of this deeply relaxed place.

Watch yourself move with the intention to hold this state of conscious resonance with your Spiritual connection for as long as possible.

Consciously make each movement—sit consciously; walk consciously. Be aware of how long and to what degree you are able to continue.

# 30  Sea of Spirit

I STAND BY THE SEA on a great expanse of sand, with rolling waves lapping gently back and forth. The sand disappears in its extension under mangrove trees that seem to be standing on stilt-like roots that plunge deep into the earth for nourishment. During one adventure in another location, a friend and I walked upon a mass of mangrove gnarls into an interior bay secluded by these trees. It was if we had been transported into another world, a world of vast unseen activity. Within this isolated landscape were nature and sea devas totally content with our being there. Not wanting to upset the balance, I was aware of my steps and movement while I curiously explored the shallow, watery world. I recall enjoying other beaches, other landscapes on both sides of various sand strips—from crashing waves created by nature's passion to bays of tranquillity where immature sharks cruised at the drop-off edge of sand and water.

The sea is a fascinating place, always different from previous visits, with various objects left for the wanderer to notice. The elements of wind and water create patterns in relation to the objects and the sand's consistency. Some beaches are packed hard enough for vehicles to drive on, others have a texture that rolls with the action of my feet when I walk. And I remember years ago when I was given a lovely book by Anne Morrow Lindbergh, *Gift From the Sea*.[27] The author shares her concepts of parallels between the ocean and our personal lives, suggesting we consider a conscious connection to life with reverence for All.

Moving within its boundaries, in sun and moonlight the sea is influenced and pulled this way and that by off-planet forces. And to realize that although it can be docilely lapping the sand, there is always unnoticed action—sand and shell being moved by currents unseen by casual observance. And there are those times when solar and lunar forces create storms expanding the sea in ferocious fury beyond the normal boundaries, forcing its water, creating alterations to large areas of coastal land, regardless of how man has attempted to construct objects to withstand its force. There are rocky coastlines where the water crashes on boulders, seemingly running into itself as it splashes spray skyward. Froth, rainbows, roaring and rumblings emanate in water's sovereignty.

This saltwater and our blood have nearly identical chemical components. Human sweat and tears contain almost the same elements as seawater. There is an exchange of energies when we are around or in the ocean. Beach excursions can seem relaxing or be very disarming. This sea is not something we control; it is far beyond what our minds can concieve. We can be in the sea physically, we can float on the surface or dive into the depths, yet we do not change the sea. It takes us into itself, surrounding us while continuing its rhythm. When we remove our physical bodies, there is no evidence that we were there. Our footprints in the sand are gone with the washing of tidal forces.

Is it any different within our own lives? Our day-to-day experiences can range from calm to raging in re-action (acting again) to forces that seem unrelated to our personal creation. Suddenly something outside ourselves happens that moves us into outrage, into compassion, jealously, empathy. How deep is our ocean? How expansive are we? Science now explores the depths of sea and space, with new 'discoveries' being made continually. As humanity we are extending our consciousness into both the complexity of our physical forms and into the depths of our Spiritual existence, into ideas and philosophies beyond previous speculation, into realms of the psyche heretofore only hypothetical possibilities. We are experiencing levels of consciousness, concepts and ideas unimagined before. Individuals have moved into similar spaces in the past, yet now scientists and psychologists are 'discovering' there is more than speculation concerning many of these avenues. Is it possible that Jesus' words, "...the works that I do shall ye do also"[28] are being fulfilled? Is it possible that we might expand our consciousness into spiritual aspects useful in assisting with such miracles? If we let go of the mass belief of God as a punisher, can we move from fear into the quality of love required to see all others as we see ourselves? So that as we come into alignment with our GodSelves, we care for others as we care for ourselves? Through the ages we have had models of loving behaviors that create waves in homes and communities, using love's influence to cleanse the sea of life. Noticeable results come from this tide moving silently within lives, creating inner action between the numerous elements of society. And there are those who have lived and/or died to create greater wave action transforming delicate patterns or intense breakers, altering mass consciousness and influencing humanity from the individual to governments.

> ✳ I experience myself as being in the expansiveness of ocean, in a place where there is no visible shore. I am on and in the sea, relaxed and supported by its warmth. I sense the smell, the fluidity as I become immersed until there is no delineation of myself. I am as an object within this mass called seawater while totally engaged within. I feel the sun, sense colors beyond the visible, hear a hum of movement with a backdrop of rhythmic clicks. Creation is enfolding me in this atmosphere. The current rocks me, while at the

same time I feel myself extend into the depths. Consciously I realize that in this moment this is real; this is all there is or can be. This expansive perception is no-thing-ness. *Isness*. This moment is All That Is. Merging into this space of allowing body sensations and movement to be entirely one with the sea presents an orgasmic expression. This might be a replica of *love*, love as a feeling without attachment to any outcome, expectation or desire —totally without ego or mind definitions. I freely float in this experience, embodying the exhilaration of these moments without regard for anything else. ✧

When we move into defining we create boxes and boundaries as the land masses do for the sea. Love flowing is as water surrounding, enveloping and permeating. All begins with the individual, with each of us in our moment-to-moment lives. We interact with ourselves reflecting every experience and person in our lives—from those in our household to those with whom we share the highways and grocery stores. Our individual undercurrents rule the wave action—from calm to electrifying. The natural inhabitants of the sea inherently create according to their specific design while human energy composites continually create from experience. Sometimes we 'spit up' something that has been buried deeply within our subconsciousness, sending it to the shore. This action ranges from the forceful to the benign— something to disgust the observer or to be found by another as riches. Many of us are now choosing to ask 'treasure' hunters for assistance in discovering things buried within the depths of our being. Why is it we want to hide these elements, even when we realize the turbulence they create? What is nourished by this obstruction? Does it serve us to transform this element of ourselves, or is it time to untangle and totally disassemble the obstruction? Restoring balance could be only a matter of seeing restrictions, noting the situation and mentally cataloging the location. The depth of our self-love is the key connection to exposing their hiding place—to disengaging, cleansing and discarding their roots in order to reveal energies that cruise through us when certain circumstances arise.

Within the complexity of our *Beingness* are connections to every interaction we ever had with ourselves and others. Agendas are the personal elements in the sea of our energy as we interact with the energetic sea of everyone in the range of our momentary encounters. There is no isolation, even when we seem to be alone on an expanse of seashore. We are the 'jewels of the sea' of humanity with every other human on the planet—the Mother Teresas and the Arafats. Just as the sea washes the sand, we are continually washed by our Spiritual connection, while we spew forth all aspects of our daily planetary existence.

The sea can rage or be placid and yet it is still the sea. It follows the energy of external forces from beneath and above the surface of its boundaries, and it is still the sea. Our energy fields are our energy fields, with the expanse being Spirit. We 'do' all sorts of things to sculpt the shores of our existence—from building walls, to creating inlets and ignoring the desolate places that are difficult to reach. Yet the Sea of Spirit, represented by our fields of Light, continues to move the grains of our sand, ever sculpting our psyches into the perfection of Spirit in the moment. Spirit has no timetable. It moves us gently. It moves us with storms of energy. And when we open ourselves to living in the moment, we remove the barriers and freely replenish our energy—just as the mangrove forest is filled in the comings and goings of tide and storm while remaining rooted in the depths of Spiritual nourishment.

# 31 Healing Our Physical Earth

I LIVE IN A SPIRIT of adventure —a passion to explore, discover, uncover, untangle and become more aware. I marvel at nature's adaptability and its resources. I love to climb, particularly rocky formations that are open enough for me to proceed safely on my own—free to establish my own routes. I know the exhilaration of standing on top of an outcropping for an expanded view. Part of me would like to hang off the side of a cliff, bouncing down the way the rappelers do.

At times I have been close to a rock when it moves or slides in a tumble down a hillside—a great reminder to stand still and anchor myself. I recall warnings some people have about earthquakes and disasters, their misgivings and the personal preparations they choose to make. The majority of earth change predictions involve massive land disasters that may or may not happen. While a client related her present fear, I read the energy surrounding her and understood one meaning. The Spirit that we are lives within a physical body composed of Earth components that frequently rumble and quake with emotional upheaval. Expressing anger nonviolently in the moment of its eruption realigns the landscape of our lives. Healing episodes can feel like earth-shattering eruptions. I held the client while she underwent major physical contractions as her energy field cleared and elevated into contentment and peace—her 'earth' quaked. Her rain of tears assisted in cleansing emotions that clouded her seeing the sun of her Being.

One morning I sat with another friend as she contemplated suicide. Her view of reality had deteriorated to where intense life examination could tip the scales either way. I listened as she talked of numerous personal scenarios that seemed out of balance and how she could see no way to bring harmony. After a couple of hours she moved into a mental and emotional clearing, processing into a form of contentment. Such energy storms wash over and through—cleansing people, things and events—presenting brighter, clearer avenues for self-expression. A conscious decision to be aware of our complete connection to Earth, to one another and to ourselves, presents awareness of how and why we are to take care of Earth—our selves, our bodies and our habitat.

The way you treat your physical bodies mirrors the way you view the Mother Earth being treated. Many see all the starvation, the humiliation, the 'natural' disasters, the whining and wailing, wanting something to be different and yet, they continue their life responses day in and day out. Others witness nature's vibrancy, love their pets and tend gardens. Notice the relationship between personal focus and physical conditions. Is illness present? For those who gripe about the condition of the water on the planet—what kind of fluids do they consume? What is the association of the physical body and the interpretation of planetary conditions?

We are not suggesting that pollution of any kind is serving anything or anyone. We are showing the reflection of humanity's carelessness of their personal physical structure to that of the Earth. Ignore any of the natural positions of either planetary or personal 'earth' and the balance deteriorates. Consider how conscientious farmers know to let the land rest. Apply chemicals to fields; apply chemicals to your body—imbalance. Cut down too many trees—imbalance. Rotate crops; rest the land. Eat healthy food; enjoy relaxation. Meditate; rest your personality. Physical capabilities are for three primary reasons—the need to eat, need for children and the need to know OneSelf. Giving, receiving and pleasure enhance each function.

Vibrations that you do not hear or see impact you unconsciously. These create energy patterns in your subtle body fields that influence the purity of your actions. Some patterns are valuable pieces of the puzzle called 'life on Earth', serving for a specific time frame or experience. After the 'job' is completed, many of these forms do not realize completion and continue their robot-like activities even when they can no longer serve you. Your conscious intervention moves these energies out of your fields to support your becoming free of pollution, and healing takes place.

As a child you discover there are times when it is best to be quiet, to do this or not do that, to restrain your natural enthusiasm. A vibration labeled 'belief' is established, reinforced by other events of similar nature particularly during adolescence. This vibratory energy continues to enforce its will in any like circumstance. Self-examination can locate these energies and let them know you have the final say in what energies are in your field. Be with your experiences while changing what prevents your highest Spiritual potential. Expand your possibilities beyond obvious solutions. ✸

Spiritual awareness knows there is more to the human body than the physical aspect. Surrounding every form is an aura, layers of energy that connect to the physical structure. Anyone can learn to feel these layers and they can be seen with clairvoyant perception. Within them are pattern sources that proceed physical discomfort and/or deformity. One can learn to 'read' the related energetics to assist in healing whatever circumstances encumber current relationships. Tracking into these places can give total release of the energy, even before it manifests physical alterations. As we deepen our awareness of such possibilities and perception of self, we can be involved with our entire energetic structure to instigate personal healing. Finding, noticing and connecting to the pattern's core is a procedure that supports opening one to receive their inherent energy to complete the related experiential Soul lesson.

Consider an analogy of storms, how they move through an area with whatever characteristics they carry—swirling and washing, blowing and lighting, transporting debris—cleansing the area and bringing in new energy. Recall the electrifying feeling when lightning charges actually change the smell of the atmosphere. So it is with our lives. Awareness happens; a gentle rain descends or a ferocious storm blows its way through our fields, altering some aspect of our lives.

Healing is an adventure into the unknown from which one returns renewed, being with all that is present—feelings, thoughts and/or pain. Changing our thoughts and beliefs alters our view of reality, however, complete healing includes perceiving related emotions. We have to be willing to feel differently about our own behavior before any lasting changes occur. Healing is not about someone manipulating events; it's our own acceptance that everything we experience is our personal reality. Others play the game to support us. Learning about the structure, makeup and purpose of our energetic bodies reveals our multidimensionality. Discovering the connection between what is actually present in relation to feelings the mind cannot comprehend establishes a greater sense of OurSelf. Respect, honor and dignity begin to radiate through life experiences.

Healing is re-uniting our perceived ideas of separation with the intrinsic God flow. Most teachings encompass looking outside ourselves to find God—a huge illusion. Religions teach the need to ask forgiveness for what we perceive we have done 'wrong,' or that we are punished by God. Yet they teach that this punishing God is all good, loving, forgiving and will continue to judge our actions. Such attempts use rationality, which confuses the 'knowingness' of our cells—*that everything is perfect in this moment.* Perhaps humanity has explored the judge premise long enough and can now embody cellular wisdom to embrace the inherent Godness of every being.

It is curious how the basis of conscious reasoning is used by Spirit to open us to opportunities. When I was first introduced to the idea of healing, my reason centered on being prepared to assist my parents should they become ill. Now years later they are in their nineties and still quite healthy. The journey has taken me from that beginning focus through exposure to many teaching modalities with numerous classmates. Perhaps it was innocence, maybe it was the consciousness at the time, however we had a common primary goal—to be a 'healer.' I learned particular hand placements that worked because certain rituals were given to me. There were specific things that had to be performed in order for healing to occur. Some think special privileges have to be granted to manifest energies necessary to assist healing.

My basic study was a holographic teaching that involved all senses with concentration on feeling since this attribute is the most repressed, disallowed and blocked in humanity. In the early '90s when I enrolled in a major healing school, I chose the teacher I felt had the highest competency level. Each student had something s/he expected to have fixed—by the teacher, by God or by our fellow class members during the proactive consultations. Gradually I discovered that although I was in the company of many who had wonderful skills, assisting was all they could do. My 'healing' was up to me. Many participants became disillusioned, even angry when these ideas surfaced. "Me be responsible? How dare you!" Some actually completed the eighteen-month school with resentment because they were not healed.

In my experience I have watched the multi-sided mental attitudes of these energies—from rebellion that you won't do it for me to accepting it is my job to heal me. And now I know the energy of empowerment. Giving our power away to others continually drains our energy, collapsing our ability to discover our greatest potential. This respected teacher never claimed that he could heal any of us. He taught self-empowerment from the start. There were personalities that continued to hold the premise that although they could empower others in their healing, they needed someone else to heal them. Healing ourselves is as important as feeding ourselves.

Enlightened healing involves being sensitive to the moment, being totally present in *Now*. Life assists by giving opportunities to see yourselves in the mirror of another person. Clean the mirror by openly looking at yourself to discover what is clouding the reflection. You have lived within this cloud haze for so long that you rarely recognize it as yours and continually project it onto someone else. Make a conscious decision to clean the mirror by moving into the depths of the cloudy source. Many, many modalities are available; some will suffice for this symptom, some for others. Yet, moving through the layers of debris hiding the base issue takes internal work within oneself. The clearing process is a conscious choice, an active expansion process to move through each encounter while staying connected to Spirit. Being open and willingly receptive are keys that lead to enlightenment.

Sovereignty happens when one takes full responsibility for self. When you want assistance, choose someone who will enhance your self-empowerment rather than someone who will interrupt this flow because they need to do something for you. The greatest healings occur by being supported through the process while each is connected to the personal GodSelf, Higher Power, HigherSelf—whatever one chooses to call this Soul aspect of themselves. Empowerment is stymied by someone's thoughts of doing it for you or by your indifference and unwillingness to fully participate in the process. Care for self; run a mile; be aware of each moment. Have a massage—stay attentive to every movement, every touch that is happening. Feel sensations and notice thoughts that arise. Realizations frequently surface anytime one is with another in a touching situation—be it the barber, the manicurist, dentist, chiropractor or lover. Choose to be conscious of what is occurring for you, not what is being done to you. Use the opportunity for self-healing and self-mastery. Claim your power.

Empowerment is not about doing for another; it is about becoming your own healer, accepting your own healership, becoming your own guru. Enlightenment is not something anyone gives you, not something you seek from another. It is moving into yourselves, into your core to recognize your own Divinity. The power of *Being* circulates through all alignments and your ability to *be*. Each of you has absolute potential, hidden only by your inability to accept Godness. Your Soul is just as good as that of any other. HigherSelf assists and directs with examples of how to live spiritually.

Enlightenment is available to anyone who chooses to discover it within. It manifests as service—service without expectation of any reward. Empowerment uses all aspects of being human, even the ego—without the ego using it. It is embodying the GodSelf, knowing the divinity of humanity, divinity of the whole. ✦

We assist in healing not only that which is present for us, but also what is present for others. There are opportunities to assist those whom we have never known. One morning before dawn I was conscious of being asleep, being totally relaxed with my body in that groovy space of heightened *Beingness* sensations. My mind clearly tracked the following experience, at times attempting to figure things out: I was involved in a healing session with a lady I seemed to know. I was being directed how to connect energies to support this healing. Particular statements were being made, particular sentiments were exchanged with information about what was happening. As this continued, a part of me realized that I didn't know this person. She agreed to assist in this demonstration of a new healing technique for me to use. The energy radiated to and permeated her, infusing cellular structure reformation, bringing balanced healing. This experience was very clear and remained in my memory when I awoke. It involved complete willingness—being tranquil, naked of personality, in nothingness, allowing and opening to being used by Spirit. I was an instrument for healing. Words cannot adequately convey this intrinsic space, a relaxed state of being Spirit.

On another occasion I was very aware that a noise triggered my consciousness. I lay completely still and observed 'pieces' of me returning to my body. They seemed to be returning from several different directions as if being drawn by me into me, 'settling in' my body, as if it were being shaken lightly by 'things' nestling into their places. All of this was real while I knew I wasn't directing any of it. It just happened and whatever it was, was exciting to watch.

I have frequently had contact with the spirits of those who have died. One morning was quite different. I sensed a 'sea' of bodies, people seeming to float aimlessly, moving to and fro by some uncontrolled force. There was no anguish, no emotion—just noncommittal moving within a sea of humanity. Faces were pallid, turned different directions. At first it was unclear if this was what some call the astral world or purgatory—or something else entirely. I asked what I was to do and received the suggestion to step into the scene.

Events happened thus:

> ❀ I am standing on something solid, like a sandbar, with Light all around me. The sea of bodies continues its movement, undulating with no focus. I ask for others to join me. I am aware of Masters, of a few people I know—we can only stand there and radiate. Those in that sea have to make the first move. It just goes on and on—people flowing by, being jostled this way and that by whatever unseen force was operating. Feelings of sadness and hopelessness permeate the atmosphere. They would rather follow than make individual moves. Then one being actually looks at me and reaches up. Only then can I reach out to this person. Immediately the color changes, pinks begin to replace the gray. This person has chosen to change. The other people seem to take no notice, and the space where one left is filled in by the moving sea of bodies. ❀

If each of us assists only one person out of that quagmire, is this enough? We can do nothing until they make a choice. I considered this episode for several days without consciously repeating it, while accepting it as a form of healing assistance. Possibly I am participating unconsciously.

Letters and phone calls come from people who tell me of my being with them—in healing sessions, dreams and meditations. My consciousness is usually unaware and I accept that such events do happen. There are many *Beings*, physical and etheric, available for consultation and assistance when we are open to their energies. I recall a gentleman telling me about his introduction to Sai Baba. He had never heard the name, knew nothing about him. In a vivid dream, Sai Baba appeared with a cognitive message that was important enough to stimulate a decision to alter his life path and travel to India to be with this teacher. Our Soul experiences are the reason for life and numerous methods are used to direct growth possibilities.

Often while in that very special morning place and energy, many visuals are present. One morning I saw a color representation of the blood stream change from red to bluish as the depleted oxygen and nutrients were absorbed, then the lungs' oxygen revitalization turned the blue to red. The pattern was the circulatory system—giving and receiving blending into the unified state of One—a life mandala. Any interruption in this divine emanation clogs not only our bodies; it reverberates to all of existence, All That Is. The flow is the Essence of Life, the mandala of creation, universal elements in unending formation and re-formation.

The experience broadened when I was instructed to face someone energetic, take their right hand in my left hand and wait. The energy influx was followed by a flow through me to them prior to a reversal. Then my right hand was placed on their chest as energy moved into my left hand, through my upper body and back to them from my right hand. As the movement continued there was a definite cleaning of the energy prior to its being returned to them. I was aware of the flow's strength, like a trickle becoming a river. Comfortable and deliberate. The visual was the circulatory system mandala—distinct light within dark while continually merging and clearing. As the heart purified, the bloodstream cleansed all cells. It takes strength in one's heart to be able to hold this, to be the chalice for such purification sequences. There was a spiral of energy set in motion as the flow in and through the other person came through my heart and returned to them. The spiraling energy moved within other spirals that included and expanded in all directions to engulf the person's *Being*.

As the process continued, their own heart energy began its flow without needing outside support and I was instructed to disconnect. This transmutation can be accomplished when we allow our chalice to be used as a distillery for the All GodEssence to unite within the two. When we interact from this deep heart space, there is a joint flow of receiving gratitude. What began as a small circle expanded into the spiral of love. I am told to use this one-on-one, physically or ethereally and to practice the process consciously until it becomes an automatic response.

During my quiet time one morning, I asked what happens to/for the receiver. Is there any consciousness of healing? I attempted to let go of what I had been taught about such concepts to be open to new interpretations.

Their conscious participation is unnecessary. Although this is accomplished within the person's Monadic/Soul levels, changes are cellular, infusing a more connected patterning into subatomic elements. Mental requirements are unneeded. The changes do filter to the physical aspect just as a raindrop becomes a trickle, a stream, an ocean. Similar action occurs with any force presenting itself to your field, whether you call it positive or negative. The energy does what it is programmed to do— nudges you, creates glitches in your feelings and expands growth opportunities by interrupting what has been present. When these energies are connected to God, this assistance empowers you to make alterations and healing occurs. All of you are repeatedly assisted in this manner, sometimes so dramatically that you term the event a miracle.

Connecting to these streams of expanded love and sharing them activates forces to integrate specifically where the receiver's fields are prepared. Noticeable changes can occur in feelings, thoughts, and/or physical conditions. Frequently someone will share a new or expanded idea that provokes contemplation and you love some circumstance that previously brought discomfort. Many times these clearings open one to face the next step with vigor and decisiveness. Recall a time when you awoke with a new awareness about something you have been puzzling over. Or a trigger pokes its head to the surface presenting another opportunity to love, another place to express gratitude for love's connection. Healing integration brings waves of creative energy into all layers of the aura and your physical body, affecting all elements of creation. Connection is enhanced with the faster frequencies, establishing a new paradigm in Earth consciousness, a new fulfillment for Essence. ✹

Our capacity to support dramatic occurrences within ourselves and Earth is supported by personal dedication and practices. As with spirals of love, openings are at first like a trickle of Light, then a headlight, a spotlight, a laser beam. Our own healing energy is strengthened by its connection to inherent Spiritual unity. Because we are in human form, sharing Spiritual Essence, all aspects of creation transform beyond limitations. Where we were unconscious before, we now recognize these streams as love. With the Soul/Heart/Earth spiral we anchor and apply healing love as our daily life. Love of Self flows in larger and larger radiating spirals, creating space in our fields for familial, communal, national and global healing. This response represents one of the ways Jesus healed—earthly expressions of total Love and acceptance of what Is.

# 32 The Play of Love

Love is organic; it is what and who we are. We love those groups and individuals with whom we feel comfortable. Any time their actions upset our ideas about life and how we live, we change our love habits. It's easy to love those who approve of us. If your love asks me to change, I question your motives. It might be easier to live without you than consider your request.

I recall my first visit to the redwood forests of northern California. Sitting at the base of one of these towering beings of lofty heights and gentle strength, I felt and imaged their acceptance of all surroundings, including me. It did not ask me to change anything; it had no suggestion as to my staying or going. It conveyed to me a magnificent inner system existing for hundreds of years, totally present in itself. Within this ecosystem every occurrence is complete Presence. Each species is protected, nourished, supported by another. Energetically we share this bond of creation; physically we contain the spiral of DNA—different combinations of the same forces creating energetic vibrations that generate our differences. This tree produces nuts; this one shade for flowers where butterflies and bees gather nectar. Here an ant colony milks aphids. Everything extends growth—these redwoods are some of the giants, filtering the exact amount of light to support various fungi and plants whose systems need less-than-direct sunlight. The symbiotic relationship of nature continually presents examples.

Can this total support and acceptance be love? In loving our neighbor as ourself, do we feed her when she's hungry? Do we support and accept him where and as he is? Does love suggest someone change?

Maybe we have only uncovered the tip of the phenomenon called love. My awareness is continually evolving, maybe yours is also. Love is fluid, without restrictions. Real love is not a quick fix. It originates from a heart aware of its inherent Goodness. It never hurts when it is presented. Love expresses in all situations and honors disagreement. Love respects limitations and holds each of us regardless of where we are or what we are doing.

We have been told that God is Love, Love is God. So what we feel as love represents our reality of God. Those whose reality (belief) is that God is to be feared because He judges, produce relationships where they are afraid of people. They may feel they can never receive approval. Those who experience outside control in their lives see their existence as a restricted environment. Wanting command of something rules their life—children, animals, bank accounts—their destiny. Some see God as allowing or supporting suffering; they might spend their lives working to alleviate suffering to the detriment of their own health—physical and/or emotional. "Love worketh no ill to his neighbor."[29]

The inherent energy of your humanity is to be the *I Am*, continually striving to express this attribute called love. One's experience of this expression is molded in the first two years of every planetary life. Whatever is the primary presentation of the child's household, presents a slanted expression of love to ego's knowing. There is a part that knows this is not Pure Love, but the personality/ego choice moves into a space of accepting these feelings as love. Your consciousness is tainted by your experiences in relationship to those around you. The Pure Love aspect is only overlaid, never altered, for who can alter God? When one makes the conscious choice to uncover and explore the layers, they can be transformed, actually changing the reality of every ego involved. ✸

Love is a tough road sometimes. Our desire to be close to others is often bought with dependency that seems viable at the time, when in reality it supports everyone's habit of searching outside self rather than discovering inner capabilities. Avoiding expectations—from anyone or anything—provides space for expanding consciousness to assist the expression of our life's evolution.

*Everything* we do, say, experience is the version of love that we have accepted. Arguments from mind/ego surface in reaction to personal encounters. Thoughts give one reality while circumstances show another. Resolution is learning to love ourselves with more awareness, thus encouraging the mind to change its identity beliefs. In every healing modality we assist others through being totally present without any need for them to change. Acknowledging the energy of "where two or more are gathered together, there will I be also"[30] calls forth tremendous nonjudgmental love and support.

Tying strings of expectation to the object of our love is a sure way to be disappointed. We ask others to love us as we are, not how they think we should or could be. Whatever we are experiencing, however we are living, is our expression of love—being love and asking for love. This is universal; it is the way we express. No matter what movies, books, counselors or anyone outside ourselves says love is, our version of love is based on our accepted beliefs.

Notice the mirrors presented through those around us—at home, work, play. Maybe it is the way someone acts, a hurtful event that triggers the mind to say there's no semblance of love.

When something doesn't feel good, we can ask to be shown how our present interpretation of love relates to the uncomfortable incident. Perhaps we want more attention or we feel unwanted. Maybe we just goofed and someone noticed—or didn't notice. How are we hiding love from ourselves? Look at how we use 'things' to show us what love is. What can we learn? How do we feel when we recognize that something or someone we have been labeling as love is not loving at all? We have to know love within before we can find it elsewhere. The part of us that is aware must impress the mind with the message that definitions have changed.

Each of us has connection to our Soul/God energies, which does know what love is, knows how to be love, how to act from love in all situations. Love is always present and we continually express it. We can be with what we think is love while setting our intention for Spirit to teach us an expanded reality of love through our experiences. The heart is where we embody this Godliness. God is Love—Love that always creates Its intentions. In order to be this Love we accept others in the same way we accept ourselves—from these same parameters we claim for ourselves. Any gifts I give to others without first receiving them myself is not "Love thy neighbor as thyself."[31]

You can each live your Divine Essence of Pure Love in everything you do, letting go of expectations, desires and definitions. Let go of past ego definitions. Move into accepting everything about you as Divine. God created everything, so everything you are is a creation of God. Let go of past; let go of any attachment to thoughts about the future. Be in the space of Now—and let go of understanding. Let go of all past feelings, wants, desires. Move into that Essence quality called God. It is always present. It has never been anywhere else. It is who you are. There has been and never will be any disconnection.

You can move into a space of nothingness where everything *Is*. This is where you feel love, you know love, you are love—at whatever level you feel it, whatever level it is known to you. Set your intention to bring this love to the surface of your experience, to open more fully, to be aware from an expanded space of consciousness, to physically embody a faster frequency, a higher vibration. ✸

How often have we packed something away and forgotten where it is or that we ever had it? Maybe we forget how to use the object. So it is with love, self-esteem, joy. They get put away or ignored until we forget these qualities that are natural aspects of OurSelves. They could be hanging close, just beyond the veil of consciousness, and we ignore them. We use this term 'love' so freely without conscious connection to its Source. Maybe its scope is impossible to grasp. Sometimes the depth of love we feel seems too much for the heart to contain. Thoughts of unworthiness surface, negating our experience. Love is vastness. Each of us has our in-the-moment capacity to give and receive in relationship to our acceptance of self-love. What I give myself, I can accept from you. From you, I can receive only that which I am willing to give myself. We continually have the opportunity to extend Source Love—the presence of Self in Love with All That Is.

When the heart is truly open there is nothing but love. It makes no difference how your mind/ego identifies it—it is the Essence of Love. As you choose to expand your awareness of Source, you can envelop everything in that love. It starts by enveloping your own self. In the times you forget about inherent love, the universe gives you experiences to reconnect, to show you "Oh, this is a place I am not expressing Essence Love." In this moment, what can you do to be all of the love expression that you can imagine? And in this moment, what can you do to be all of the love expression you can know? Love owes no one. Love leans on no one. Love demands of no one. Love allows expression of everything without criticism or judgment, while at the same time recognizing ways to *Be* personal love expressing.

It would assist many to evaluate their possessions, noticing the energy being presented by things. These hold energies of the past, re-minding your mental states of old patterns, memories, collections of outdated thoughts—even those considered positive. Holding onto these things tends to cloud your activities, making it more difficult to discern momentary decisions. It's like having to please a whole committee on every detail. These belongings re-present their energy, leading you down a stale path that includes them—frequently quite disruptive—rather than your own unique journey.

It is important to notice what is out of sync, particularly in your sleeping and eating spaces. Purging these spaces of anything representing outdated energies is advisable to keep harmonic balance. The third dimensional reality that humanity is experiencing, puts up with much more baggage than does the faster vibrational levels most of you are establishing in your systems. Whatever level you know love to be right now will change, grow and expand. The frequency becomes faster and faster. Encourage and support yourself being the love you are in all personal activities.

This Love is your birthright. It is who you are. It is what Earth is. It is what the Universe is. The stars are made of this. The Purity of Love is God. No matter how it is experienced, how many contradictions appear, everything is still God, Source, Creator. It is the energy with which you create your lives. Partake of it fully. It continually radiated in Jesus' life. With the vibrations of Earth at that time, there were those few followers who could believe this Kingdom of Love was possible.

In the Earth's vibrational fields today, as you open to love, greater things are happening. You are part of it, whether you choose to or not—just because you are physical. It is why you are here, to be aware and conscious of present possibilities. Give yourself the gift of knowing and sensing your Love Essence. ✸

Ideas, concepts and experiences of spirituality are difficult to express without using comparisons—references based in duality—until we truly embody and live the feelings of expansion and freedom. The term 'unconditional' love is only an idea of a possibility. In actuality, *love is*—it is never conditional so it cannot be unconditional. Love is feeling, undefinable with words. Being cannot be defined. Thinking about hows and whys and whats brings confusion and invalidation, continuing comparison. The Essence quality structures of Spirit, God, Creator, Source, All That Is are known through feeling, through perception from the place of *Beingness*. A part of me must perish to reach Heart Love. Everyone expresses aspects of God from within and as we move into greater love within our hearts, we connect with the Beloved, an aspect of God referred to as the Christ Consciousness. Living more fully from this Presence expands the God qualities within. From here I see others without reaction. From a deep compassion and caring, Goodness reigns as the Pure Love of God within me. In seeing God as and in everything, I can support others from this love, while at the same time choosing to move beyond the veils, attitudes, experiences of seeming separation. This is through the lesser, denser energies that are also God without heart expression. As we share love with another, we are God loving God from our present personal connection to this Goodness.

❧ I am overlooking a bay. Life teems in, above and around this water. I am shown this as love, as what is present in any moment—fluid, holding, contained, supporting, nourishing, ebbing—current totally in its *being* water, unconcerned and encompassing aliveness. This is a reflection of embodying the fluidity of God, the vessel we call Soul and HigherSelf as encouraging and nourishing, supporting the ebb and flow of all life. Our Soul is in relationship to God as we are to our HigherSelf. Our Soul knows there is more and goes with this and that experience, searching for the right combination to its beginning. Jesus, Buddha, the Masters show us the way and we keep experiencing and expressing, looking for the key that zooms us to God. Source continually sustains us without any judgment or expectation, and we continue living life. ✎

When we set our intention to accept spirituality and open to the Essence energy of Love, the expression is awesome. Love is a discovery, an adventure with no definition. If God is Love, is All That Is every love expression of life we encounter regardless of our belief? What if *being love* is passionate aliveness—being comfortable doing exactly what we are doing, being who we are? The only way we can know love and expand its qualities in our lives is to realize its influence as we share with others. The act of sharing and giving keeps these attributes polished and shining, reflecting our inner development.

What matters is how love pours through us and how we open to learning All That Is about love in this moment. It's about moving deeper inside to discover the guru within. It's how love is expressed through each of us, how we perceive God expressing through us. There are always outside things to distract our attention, while at the same time we are reflecting what is within by how we place our attention on external affairs. There are circumstances that seem detrimental while everything is in perfect order. From the place of the greatest love that each individual can touch, may we passionately uphold the highest good for everyone and everything in Creation—regardless of what it is, regardless of how it seems to be manifesting. No one thing will evolve any faster than the whole. We are all in this together. My prayer is that each of us opens ourselves to our Selves to bring Love into reality in everyday affairs.

# 33  Meditation to Connect Love

THIS MEDITATION enhances a deeper consciousness of the inherent Love that we are. Be sure to set aside time for yourself to do this—a minimum of 15 minutes, preferably thirty minutes.

Sit in a comfortable position; breathe easily and notice your body as you move into your relaxation, a place where you feel safe and loved. ❁

Breathe deeply, inviting your Guardians and supporters to be present. ❁

Welcome the energy of Christ Consciousness, Pure Light. ❁

If you choose, include the group energy of the Masters and Archangels. ❁

Notice your physical body, scanning through the body to see what's present. ❁

Become aware of Earth, looking at the dirt, the rocks, the water. See a place with plants, with growth and abundance. ❁ ❁

Move your attention to the willingness nature exhibits to share its Essence, its balance. ✸

Be in acceptance of physicality, aware of your connection to Earth and all that it is—in whatever state it appears. ✸

Concentrate your awareness on the connection of the physical body with Earth. Your physical form doesn't exist anywhere else, only on this planet. ✸✸

Continue to be aware of your body as you move your attention to your heart. ✸

Connect with the energies that are pouring through your heart, the place of Love from Source. Then ask the Soul/HigherSelf connection to Source to expand this area more than ever. ✸✸

Now ask this connection to move through your body. ✸✸

If there is any place of resistance, breathe love into that place. ✸✸

When the heart is truly open there is nothing but love. Your mind/ego identity makes no difference—it is the Essence of Love. ✸

Begin to track this love into the cellular structure, into every molecule of your body, ✸

Through the atoms, protons—whatever name your mind knows, ✸✸

All the way into the DNA structure, the part of you that recognizes love and is able to bring love to the surface. ✸✸

Love assists awareness, moving in and through as body sensations. ✸

Fill your body with this love. ✸

And fill your aura. ❀

As your body is filled with it, you can sense the bodies of others filled with it. ❀❀

Feel this communication and watch it change and expand. ❀❀

Source Love is your birthright. It is who you are. ❀

The Purity of Love is God.

Breathe it in, as much as you choose to absorb. ❀❀

Partake fully, using your breath to expand it, being aware of your experience. ❀❀

You might hear sounds; you might see colors, sense colors. ❀

Make it as real as you choose. ❀

Buddha modeled this Love. It is the energy Jesus knew.

Be aware that between the thoughts, in that no-mind space, is communication with the Beings of Light and Love. ❀

In silence ask your HigherSelf to direct your heart energy for the maximum experience.

Set your intention to stay in this Heart Essence. ❀❀❀❀

(If you are creating a tape of this, allow five to ten minutes of silence before continuing.)

Slowly become aware of your physical body, noticing any feelings, any sensations. Whatever thoughts pop into mind, welcome them as part of right now, this Divine moment. ❀❀

Breathe from your heart into Earth and back to your heart. ❁ ❁

Take three deep breaths as you return your attention to your body position and support. ❁

Slowly and gently move your fingers, feet, legs; begin to stretch. ❁

Open your eyes, keeping them defocused as you begin to be aware of your surroundings. ❁

Gradually become totally conscious of where you are and how you feel, thanking all who participated in your experience.

## 34 Creating Beyond Beliefs

Do we seriously consider anything beyond our beliefs? Those of us who believe in leprechauns open our fields for their response, thus we can see them. Inventors have a sense of their finished product, thus inviting the energies necessary for production to show themselves. Before Henry Ford devoted himself to the automobile, he built watches, estimating he could manufacture them by the millions to sell at about thirty cents each. Since he thought people would never need to own one, he didn't go into the business.

We struggle to define the present from past beliefs, confining our reality to what we are told is possible. The consciousness we hold is the way we see ourselves and others. "What you see is what you get." "What I believe is what I get." All of us are artists re-creating the present—ours and that of past generational influences. Any change activates thoughts about survival and safety, rarely incorporating feelings of love. Memories program our reactions until we alter our beliefs—always given to us by others. As we change our defense responses, we release constrictions in our life spirals, enabling us to contact pure Creation. Know ourselves and be free. Isness activated.

Suspending dis-belief to consider the holographic perspective of all things, visions and sensations, allows them to teach us truth. As holograms of the Creator we have all the attributes of the Creator and exist in all dimensions. When we experience a thunderstorm with lightning and noise, we connect to particular words and various emotional experiences. One person might stand in awe of the experience; another might hide in the closet. One night a friend who was staying with me found herself standing in a doorway during a minor earthquake. Her inner voice aroused her from deep sleep, quickly moving her in response to her childhood conditioning. All responses are energetic replies to particular thoughts, feelings or emotions. The storms themselves are not a creation of our reaction; they care not how we feel or think about them.

Every idea hangs in the ethers until someone adds his energy, similar to stillness in the leaves of a tree until a puff of breeze creates movement. Some folks choose to sit back and let life live them in some pre-existence, repeating their story of the past in today's circumstances. Others recognize possibilities, notice intentions and continually choose to *be* Presence. Because of ingredients and circumstances in the moment, what is available now is all that can manifest. Change just one particle and another scenario happens. We can only be where we are, who we are *Now*. If this is not satisfying, it is my choice to alter *my* involvement with no attempt to change that of another. We are these continually changing bodies, thoughts and ideas—both physical and spiritual.

Until we add intention, ideas continue to float hither and yon. Intention grabs the idea. Wanting it to materialize in this way and not that way hampers the universal scheme of support. Notice the intent and be present for directions as to the next step. Do what is relevant in the moment and let go of pushing for anything else. Being willing and available to follow these inclinations is instinctual doing rather than manipulating production. Let go of all definition, all connection to if or how or when. Universal energy has more for us than we can imagine.

When one responds from the attitude of, "Well, let's get this over with," personal perseverance tightens the muscles, triggers an adrenaline wash and closes the heart. Steps that would assist are ignored or forgotten so any accomplishment materializes slowly. If the project is ever finished, those involved are frequently grumpy, angry or belligerent. Not a loving way to treat your bodies, to work or run a business. Continually expand your consciousness within the scope of self-directed action that supports self in all aspects. Empower actions in all realms—speech, thoughts, job-related activities, play, eating, hygiene, spending, giving, asking. Embody your own transformation—enlightenment in action. It's living with what *Is* in this moment, accepting Divine support in every endeavor.

Play with this exercise:

❧

Think of something you would like to have in your life.

What do you think has to change for this to happen?

If this were to happen, what changes would occur?

Are you willing to make these changes?

How would life appear if you totally lived in *Now* allowing the present to unfold the future? ❧

How one feels moment to moment is being conscious of all present creative elements. If we recognize joy, this situation is satisfying; if there are unwanted ingredients, it is up to each of us to choose differently. Move somewhere else. Do things another way. We are the creative force manifesting everything in our lives—that which we believe to be true. Feeling we are forced or trapped gives our power to some external circumstance. Flow with vulnerability; feel the loneliness, the exhilaration and the walls.

When there is lack (a filter clouding pure vibration), we manifest on that level. Gratitude triggers the I Am presence of divine truth, which demonstrates materialization as our divine right. It is our Soul in action. Real manifestation contains joy. It isn't something we have to work for. It isn't something we have to do. It's the state of being our Essence. When we experience the truth of our hearts, we connect to unified dimensionality. This space is a knowing beyond belief, a sensing of our divine right as present reality.

Internal honesty is integrity every moment, expressing every truth. And when each of us is in this space, sharing is without words—energy moving through us while sustaining our individual excitement. When I am conscious of my connection to Source I feel joy, gratitude and expansion. My energy seems to flow out like that of an egg being cracked open. In unity there can be no expansion or contraction. Those are perceivable only by the mind in justification. Contraction regurgitates the past. Expansion is freedom into feeling all dimensions with no reference to what can or has happened. Oneness is felt in the moment. This keeps the vehicle vibrating as a spiral—similar to a tuning fork, ever enveloping its vibrational pitch, thus creating new energy dynamics—manifestation.

Until we get it that there just might be another way and that *we deserve to liveproductive and happy lives,* we are ignorant of the possibilities. It's not about digging deeper, learning more, looking somewhere else. It's about being willing to see from a different perspective, to experience differently. Sleep on the other side of the bed, drive another route to work, eat lunch at a new restaurant. Quit doing the same things the same way. Everything is as we have chosen it to be. We think, feel, act, and it is so.

My Guides suggest that I be wary about following anyone who says they have the only way, know the way for me—

whether this be a physical being, a spirit or a guide. Unless they emphasize adventuring into our own truth, they tend to control our lives superficially. Be excited, enthralled, captivated without becoming attached to any particular person, ideology, or manner of self-acceptance. Others can only point out their concept. I find what's best for me right now. You find what's best for you. This can change next week, next year. We are here to assist one another in the search while not expecting anyone to even think about walking our path. Meditate, consider and integrate that which serves, following our own HigherSelf guidance. Wherever you are right now, I respect that place. Each of us can paddle the same lake, in the same area, but each of us has our own canoe. Let us honor ourselvesand respect ourselves for what we have done. Manifest now, not yesterday, not tomorrow, right *Now*.

I have experienced and observed with friends that as we become less attached to everyday life, the results of our intentions manifest more freely. When a direction is presented, act upon this idea, holding the complete intention without any attachment. Let the Universe negotiate the outcome. Use intuitive imagination to open into Soul, into Its listening to God, into being in the silence of ourselves, disconnected to outcome, detached from doing. Infinite possibility is not about getting something; it is being in the flow of co-creation in the moment— it demands our attention. Abundance is being able to do what we intend to do while flowing in the law of balance—the circulation of giving and receiving. It takes loving ourselves *as we are right now* to clearly accept that no matter how the original idea is represented, it is the perfect combination for this moment. We can choose to follow intuitive directions with trust in the outcome and open to the presentation of God's sources.

 To Source, the experience of your lives is your donation of sharing God's Love. Only when you pay for something grudgingly do you change this natural structure. It puts the squeeze on the energy. Freely give of your Self—all of you, every aspect of you; tithe your Beingness. This expands that beginning step of giving a percentage of your income, to generosity—giving without any attachment, desire, want or request. Remember there can be no separation between this and that, between money and time, between smiles and frowns—the natural rhythm of creation and re-creation. When you purchase anything, be aware of all the resources necessary to bring the product to you. Connect to the creative energies used to re-source it, mold it into this particular form. Consciously play with these traits of self-empowerment to initiate the ecstasy of Creation.

This is our life, our growth, our consciousness. Honoring ourselves and everything around us gives us the experience of the only God we know. The flow with the rhythm of Creation contains an agreement that every action is heart-centered as we follow the mandate of our Soul's experience to know through feeling the *Am* of I Am. We are the abundance of God continually filling with life.

One of my experiences with this came while busily packing supplies at the end of a ministerial class. One of the participants approached to say good-bye, handing me a check. We shared hugs and appreciation, continuing with our individual activities, I temporarily put the check in my camera case. In bed that night I thought of her and the gift she had given, realizing she was tithing to one of the sources of her spiritual inspiration. This awesome awareness evoked my deep gratitude for this gift. The next morning when I stopped at a roadside park that overlooked a large bay, I retrieved the gift. Tears immediately began to flow. I walked to the water's edge, part of me berating myself, thinking I hadn't thanked her properly. I sat on a rock, grieved, released guilt, and was astonished and elated. I remembered she was going to visit her daughter before returning home. I couldn't even call her. I sat in silence, listened and watched—the scenery and myself until my derriere was numb.

Continuing my journey, I recalled a well-stocked bookstore in a town I would pass that just might have a book I'd been unable to locate. At one of the highway exits I called the store and learned they had one copy. I asked the clerk to reserve it for me at the front desk. When I walked into the store, my mouth dropped open, quickly moving into a huge smile. There at the checkout counter stood my friend and her daughter, who lived in a nearby town. They were just leaving the store. Any additional stops or any abbreviation of my route would have prevented this manifestation. She was as amazed as I. Why were either of us in this town? In this store? The combination of my thoughts, intent and emotional feelings became the essence of creation with no consideration on my part. Let go and let God.

People who have had near-death experiences seem to report similar experiences and questions asked of them while they were in that other space. "How did you use your gifts in contribution to people and the world at large?" "What did you learn about love?" Trust in love and joy as natural attributes of our Soul. In these expressions we become all the abundance we can use and give away. As we interrupt the ways we perpetuate outdated beliefs, we become immersed in life, opening ourselves to flow in the reverence of everything available—the fluctuations, the rhythm of creation—without any grabbing or holding. We attach to nothing and joyfully express abundant love through all interactions, no matter what the task.

The nature of God is absolute good(ness). In no way can we impinge upon this truth, regardless of our beliefs. Everything is always available; nothing is kept from us. We set our intentions and let go. We follow intuitive urgings with love for every encounter. We ask and it is provided. Or it just appears. Or we twitch our nose and it's present. The flow of who we are includes perfection. We create life as expanded gifts of Divine Love flowing effortlessly in the interaction of one another's GodHood.

> One day the abbot gave his monks a sieve and told them to fill it with water. They were perplexed. They sat in contemplation. Each held it, turned it and thought some more. How could they possibly accomplish this task? They pondered, experimented and finally told the master it was an impossible assignment. The master smiled, took the sieve and began walking slowly and deliberately. He looked out over the lake. Then he threw it in the lake. The monks watched in comprehension as the water immersed the sieve; *it was filled with water!*
>
> *A Zen story*

# 35 Meditation for Personal Awareness

Jesus, Buddha, Mother Teresa, and Krishna, among others, have been examples of enlightenment while living in human form. Each of us can choose to learn for ourselves where that space of *Beingness* is and how it can manifest through us. We possess a unique aspect of Creation. We have a physical form to move in this world. We have a Spiritual Self, the *I Am* presence that seeks expression.

Use this exercise to reflect places where you are holding back. Choose a time and place when you will not be interrupted for at least twenty minutes. Read slowly, allowing feelings to surface. Notice particular suggestions that you respond to intensely. Use deep breaths from Source to shift these feelings. Later you might want to note these for deeper healing.

൦ჯ

Relax wherever you are, being conscious of the body, leaving the mind in its wandering. ✹

Set your intention to stay with your feelings, noticing the personality whenever it jumps in, while exploring your re-actions to the following.

Look at how it feels when everything doesn't go just as you want it to in your life—when things don't work out just the way you planned: ❀ ❀

…When someone doesn't do what you feel they ought to do. ❀ ❀

…When you are disappointed about something that has happened. ❀ ❀

You are a good person. Why do bad things have to happen? ❀

How does it feel when you hear of children being abused? ❀

How does it feel when things happen that you have nothing to do with, and yet you are in the middle? ❀ ❀

You're driving down the road; minding your own business and are interrupted by someone unexpectedly hitting your vehicle. ❀ ❀

…To have friend, who are jolly, doing what they want to do, and suddenly they die. ❀

…To watch family, friends and other people with disease, their bodies racked with pain, still be here for whatever reason. ❀ ❀

Do you get upset with God because that Creator Energy allows these things happen? ❀

How would it look if each of us were God? ❀

Would you have such events in this human experience? ❀ ❀

How might your life be if these events were your responsiblity? ❀ ❀

How would it feel? ✹✹

What is it in you that thinks you could do a better job than God? ✹✹

Give you the control. You can make it work. ✹

Feel this idea. ✹✹

Is there is a voice that says, "Yes, I can make it work." ✹

Is there a voice that says, "No! I don't want that responsibility."? ✹

Is there a voice that says, "What can I do?" ✹

What would it take for you to be someone with so much love that others would feel the experience of love through you? ✹✹

With this love flowing through you, could you possibly affect the way the planet is? ✹

Do you want to be that effective? ✹

How might Jesus support you in such love? ✹

By going about doing His own thing, ignoring things going on around Him? ✹

How might Buddha support you? ✹✹

Be aware of your responses—feelings, body sensations, thoughts. Just invite them to be present without needing to do anything about any of this. ✹✹

Experience letting go of all thoughts right now. ✹

Feel Love within you. Breathe into that space as if blowing on an ember. ✹

Breathe it into a flame. ✹

Breathe it into a fire, bigger and bigger—a fire of clarification. ❀❀

This fire will help purify any space within that is ready to change. ❀

Breathe this flame in; ask it to cleanse whatever space wants to be cleansed. Specify places if needed. ❀❀

(For some, this fire could also be coming up through the feet.)

Ask that the love you know be expanded and expanded. ❀

Forgive yourself for forgetting who you are. ❀❀

Look within to see what it might take to be in the space of Pure Love that you know you are. ❀❀

If any obstacles come up, breathe the fire into this space. ❀

You can send this love, this fire of love to those whom you know are hurting. ❀❀

Express your gratitude to you for participating in this experience. ❀

Now bring your attention to your body, scanning your body to recognize all the feelings. ❀

Notice whatever is happening. ❀

Be aware of where you are. ❀❀

Take two deep breaths, gradually opening your eyes, becoming focused in this present moment. ❀ ❧

# 36  Responding to Life

THE BREAKUP of my twenty-five year marriage was a tremendous blow to my I-know-how-things-are-supposed-to-be ego. Togetherness, children, adventures and fun characterized the experiences of those years. It seemed we were well on our way to manifesting all our shared dreams when the flow was interrupted. A huge energy, unimaginable to me, energy planted itself within our picture—my husband wanted to play with someone else. For months I spent every waking moment attempting to solve the puzzle of how and why, using inner contemplation, reading, listening and talking with loving mentors. I realized I knew myself only as a mother or wife who had a strong connection to continuing the status quo.

Diligently I prayed for his return and to my surprise, he did. My basic prayer was answered. I was elated and grateful. Five months later we both knew the act being played out had three discordant realities—his, mine and ours. It was a painful time, but the intensification propelled each of us into a whole new venue of life. We were each fortunate to have experienced these productive years of family life with its upsets, fun and challenges. Although unrealized then, I now see the defensive tactics we used to justify our momentary stances—accusing, blaming, choosing allies. One of the statements I recall him saying was, "Someday you will thank me for this." This possibility was completely out of my reality. Fourteen years after our divorce, I took the opportunity to thank him personally, for I have wondered how Spirit would have directed me to be where I am now without this breakup.

Most of us can look 'back' to milestone events in our lives, many considered 'normal'—first grade, graduation, college, marriage, births and deaths. Other personal events hold individual significance—illness, divorce, poignant deaths. Many events and things influence who we seem to be and how we live our lives. I am grateful, not necessarily for painful experiences, but for opportunities and people who have been and are part of my life today. On this ever-changing road, *Now* is timeless perfection. It's as if my picture of reality correlates to a puzzle with all its pieces in a pile. Here and there pieces fit together and more come into organization to support my sorting through momentary reality. Here and there I find something that relates to a previous understanding, thus beginning a series of leads that produce a shift in consciousness, allowing more awareness in the puzzle of *me*. This moment builds on this moment, this experience and this revelation—perfection in its continual unfoldment.

How often are we like a circular staircase—reaching from here to there in a manner never before experienced? In the original building process of the Sisters of Loretta Chapel in Santa Fe, New Mexico, the contractors forgot the stairs to the choir loft. Legend says a man appeared one day, saying he knew he could build the needed stairs as a spiral structure. He had never done such a thing before. In fact, he had never even seen one or had considered such staircases previously. Today the actuality of this spiral staircase still defies building forms—no nails, no structural support. Are we willing to be an unsolved puzzle in our own life? Look for the times in life when we have found ourselves in situations with the opportunity to give up or move forward—frequently minus tangible support. A commitment to all facets of life that keep our personal spiral supported, disallowing the return to the circle continuum.

How powerful this can be when we also let go and open our senses to receive other stimuli to deepen our spiritual experience in the moment. At times we are suddenly aware of having missed an opportunity to respond with greater inclusiveness. Moments of revelation are not the time to berate ourselves, rather to celebrate that we notice our lack of previous awareness and make decisions for our involvement from an expanded viewpoint. Soul is the instigator of experience without any agenda as to how or when we experience each piece of the puzzle in the development of ItSelf.

There are multilevel aspects of creating our reality—our physical world being the one that we give the most attention. Additionally, there is our perceptive reality based upon what the mind believes—beauty, fear, power, disappointment, personal worth, age, etc. One day something happens in our life to activate an idea from the mental storehouse and wham-o—an automatic response of our egoic self. Suddenly we are in an encounter without being conscious of any steps we took to get there. What just happened? We can shake our heads, count to ten, cry or have a tantrum. How we react to various stimuli is based upon the interaction between our personality and our SpiritualSelf. The mind issues plans. Our emotional reality expands with joy and happiness or retracts in fear or pain. Or we connect to Love using this spiritual stimulation for personal growth and illumination.

One cannot separate the flesh of a leaf from the veins and still have a healthy leaf. You cannot divide yourselves and live your most fulfilled lives. So to avoid unpleasantness, pain and sorrow, you shut out parts of yourselves, thinking you are whole when in fact you are existing as fragments. You know fear and power and love. Yet you seemingly deny one to be another. You flatten yourselves into little coins of existence when you could experience yourselves as a whole universe. You think you can squeeze yourself into this or that hole to hide and watch, being part of life without participating fully. Each of you made the choice to return to Earth for specific experiences and when you attempt to take yourself out of your own life you discredit the natural process of being human. You unconsciously rob potentiality in the moment, thus restructuring your next experience into a new scenario of evolvement and its perfect expression. You serve yourself in your highest form of creation by being aware in every instant. Your Soul experiences are fully empowered. You are the whole of yourself. ✸

Frequently we see a narrowly focused sector of life. Our schedules entail a routine for five days and another for two days. This must be done Monday, this on Saturday. Do this only at such and such store, drive those streets to get there. And if some obstruction is presented, frustration jumps right up with a confused reality. The picture of today suddenly changes—our physical world looks different. Feelings surface to counteract the change. The brain stimulates the adrenal glands, fear stresses the muscles, the blood pressure elevates and the mind goes into spasms of 'what if,' 'do this,' 'go this way'—triggering feelings that can be totally irrelevant to the situation, creating a reality completely out of context with the facts.

"The boss wants to see you." Brain goes, "Oh my, what have I done?" Typically questions arise, followed by fear. The adrenals open and the nervous system restricts blood flow to the brain, pumping more blood into the muscular system. This redistribution restricts mental capabilities, creating fuzzy thoughts while preparing the body for physical activity. All of this occurs within seconds of the original message that the boss requests our presence—perhaps to give praise for our latest accomplishments. Once I had a similar reaction when I saw a flashing blue light behind me on a highway—the officer told me a brake light was malfunctioning.

Years of reinforcement frequently entangle the attributes of fear and excitement. To check your experience, explore with this exercise, looking at a personal fear episode and sensing your body sensations.

❧

Recall an event where you felt fear.

Be totally aware of how you feel when you recall this fearful episode.

Notice any physical tension , muscle tightening, your breathing.

Does your heart rate increase?

What voices do you hear?

Now relax into the present. Be with yourself.

Note any pictures, ideas or thoughts, and relax beyond these. Let them float naturally in your consciousness.

Now recall something exciting, a happy time when you were involved in a joyful experience.

Notice all the body sensations associated with excitement—tension, heart rate, breath, thoughts.

Relax again, remembering these feelings.

Put these two episodes side by side to examine the energies. Are there similar or different body sensations in fear and excitement?

Notice any contrasts in emotions and thoughts.

Do you discover related feelings in each scenario?

Does the body seem to function the same in either situation?

What does this tell you? ∞

Every aspect of reality is cooperating beyond our consciousness, many times in ways that we would not mentally choose. We move through our days from this activity to that, with detached observation, unaware of our Selves and the interaction. We have spent years perfecting our physical makeup—looks, dress code, ways we present ourselves in various situations. We pay very little attention to what or who has influenced our choices. Am I my parents? Teachers? Spouse? When and why do we present this or that mask? Society says we should do this in this manner. How does this serve us? What does our total Self say?

The only way to change this course is to be conscious of the situation and all aspects. This change begins at the physical level—breathe deeply, relax and check out all feelings. Allow the mind to recognize current facts, feelings—and then act consciously. Healing comes with awareness, an aspect of our God connection. Re-form our puzzle by the piece or in groups of colors. As each is presented in its rightful place, clearing happens, activating movement of the spheres. Consciousness expands, Soul energies rush in to wash and cleanse. The vibration of the physical vehicle elevates, altering life's course. The body responds with the energy of love for Self.

∞

Play with this exercise:

Take yourself to a personal experience involving many people on a joyous occasion.

See the place, the people. Feel the energy, the collaboration of everyone having a good time.

Notice your own energy, your connections, your participation.

Now disengage from this scene.

Breathe deeply, really feeling yourself with awareness.

Return to that place as it is now—empty. You are there alone. What is this awareness?

How does it compare to the previous experience?

Check out the reality you are creating in this moment.

Does it reflect or depend upon your memory of another time?

Or can you be comfortable with the physical reality that is present now?

What if the past experience had been unpleasant?

Do you feel threatened or could this empty place be soothing?

All that is there is a physical place that re-minds you of another time, presenting different realities, triggering various emotions and thoughts.

It is up to you to choose re-action or new action. ❧

We can look at our lives as a theatrical production, be it drama, comedy, opera or tragedy. We are the producer, director and star. To some extent we choose the script and numerous people are drawn to our production—as cast and audience. Our play contains the production of everyone else—plays within plays. The scripts merge and clash in their interaction. It's when we fail to notice these scenes are interactive that we get caught up in resistance to having some person upstage our production. Without this continual interchange we would be alone on our stage without even an audience. Life is not designed that way, nor would opportunities be present for our growth.

When the interaction gets too hectic we attempt to either abandon our play to become involved in the play of another, or we leave this stage to reopen our preformance somewhere else. However, we take our play with us and find others willing to play with us while their own production continues. Anything left unfinished has to be completed someday, so eventually we find ourselves back in the same old drama with a different cast, layout and audience.

A group of family or friends decide to play in a variety of experimental experiences. Everyone decides where they would like their exploration to begin and what they would like to experience. One goes to China, another to Brazil, another to Washington. One wants to participate in experiences, not places, so s/he chooses food, plants, mountain climbing. One decides to look through microscopes for things previously unseen, another decides to study the stars. Each has choice about their equipment, their time frame. They commit to regrouping after certain things have been accomplished, and they excitedly disperse into their chosen explorations.

After a while, they are so involved that their memory of the original decision to regroup is beyond recall. At some point, however, there is a stirring. It may be piqued by meeting someone unknown, yet familiar. There may be a lull in their lives and they feel an urge to alter the course they have followed for years. Something occurs to stimulate an unconscious desire to regroup. Everyone begins to return, to unite as old friends sharing experiences. Each discovers that individual lives have been enhanced by one another's explorations via inventions, discoveries, literature. They realize they have influenced each other's lives *without even knowing some of their counterparts who contributed to this play*.

Such is the play we call humanity. Acts are completed and sets are changed for the next scene. Every part of my play and the interaction with yours is perfection right now, no matter what is happening. A theme completes and we construct another. Topics are similar based on the structures of human life and sudden interventions such as illness or divorce. We can counter the overall directive and run things our way, follow, lead or sit on the sidelines. God gives total permission to do whatever. We learn the results of one action and decide how to do it another way, always searching for and learning to express love.

Themes held by our Soul's purpose continue to be part of the production until we have no charge on any outcome, until we can hold Love for all through every scene. Interchanges include primary interactees and numerous supporting or interfering energies. Awareness notes our actions while consciously we see only minute glimpses of the total play. Attuning to sovereignty presents opportunities to be completely involved in and yet be detached from *any* outcome or change in script, in actors or directors. We flow in the moment, continually ad-libbing to the occasion. Our lives are the quest of our Soul Director. My visualizing the Soul Directors of every actor in my play activates gratitude that I have only my part to play. Wanting it to be otherwise is saying the Master Director doesn't know what S/He is doing. "Why don't you just let me direct my life? I know what is best for me." Another part of me knows the truth.

Notice the multiple 'stages' under Soul's direction and accept ourselves as bit players for just so long before evolving into the main character. The goal is to become the hero/heroine who completes this stage and moves on. Following external directions can detour this unique journey. Discomfort, though it may be intense, signals that perhaps our change in direction is less than positive for our production. Uncompleted cycles leave gaps. We can perceive a connection between this experience and that encounter and consider the perfection of being in these places, at this time, at this particular age. We can choose to portray our particular character so fully that we are completely immersed in evolution with astonishment and wonder. We live fully *just to be totally present.* This moment is all that is preordained. This moment is perfect. Everything about it is exquisite.

As awareness elevates, other experiences are available—rain falls, a creek swells, it might even exceed its banks. Where vegetation has been on solid ground, now it's flooded—different aspects are present. Such are our ideas, concepts and truths about experiences. Accept another possibility and the experience overflows with new developments. I create my reality—everything I see and interact with. I live in a certain place and in this way because my thoughts have produced it. Even when my consciousness cannot connect to reasons why this or that is happening, I accept that I create my portion. If you are involved, you are also a creator of this interaction. The community, country, the mass population of the world plays its part.

Since choosing to consciously attend to my spiritual growth, many avenues have been presented. I live a full life with varied experiences. I follow and explore invitations—some seem insignificant while others have propelled me for long periods of time. Responses to life flow in and out and up and down, anchoring, expanding the spiral of life. When I notice that I feel motionless, I look for obstructions. Many times I'm dragging my feet, not wanting to let go to move ahead. I might find someone or something energetically holding me. None of these situations is productive. I must move freely. If I stay in one place, with one group, teacher, book, ideology, beyond the place of maximum potential, my evolving growth is stifled. Any of us can allow information to become a box in our reality that takes away the joy of exploration.

If identity is based on past boxes of the mind we can never recognize who we are in this moment. I have been told I am very eclectic. Such ideas represent the speaker's reality. If I attempt to be what someone else thinks I am, I move out of experiencing me. Many parts of me gather as if for a ruling. My personality/ego either denies or inflates, or the message may come, "If this is the true, then let's get out there and really *be* this." Ideas of other people are sometimes a projection of their reality or an attempt to program me to fit into their ongoing stage production.

When presented with another's ideas of who we are, we can think about it, feel it, discard it or live it fully. Ideas can move through us or we can become attached to them. *It is up to us.* Ego might do one thing to play out its scheme; mind would do another. Some part wants to talk about it; another part says, "Be still. Wait." Mind pulls us to categorize and summarize all the fors and againsts. Tightening comes when one takes someone else's idea and owns it without looking at how or if the associated connections fits present personal identity. Accepting projected ideas becomes a band that continues to tighten, thus squeezing our reality into that shape rather than our being free within reality's ebb and flow. Be *You now* as Soul.

The perception of others makes no difference. IAm *is* in this moment. It's a strange feeling—to be this Soul center *and* all other aspects at the same time—like one big circus that has very little to do with 'if I am.' Examining 'someone thinks I am' is an opportunity to feel my ideas about who I am without going outside myself for definition. This connects to inherent Goodness, a connection to every thing, a free-ness of being—mine and theirs. When I set my intention and ask for guidance and assistance, I broaden this stream, freeing myself of past bonding.

 ⚘ My heart expands. My field brightens, becoming

rainbow flecks inside a sphere of free-flowing fluid, undulating, without pattern. My breathing is slow, deep, relaxed. I am aware of worldly activity around me while being this sphere. My eyes glaze, drift, close, see without concentration. It is safe to be in this connected place while being me. There are tingles. I can do physical things and keep this expansiveness. This is my life. I imagine I am this totally free being. Just how would this aspect live? Would anything be different in my daily life? This is who we are—each of us. We are living expressions of comprehensive expansion. An hour ago I was engrossed in something else, yet did I completely leave this space? We never leave this space. It is our Essence. Learning to be aware of moving and doing while being connected to this consciousness is my intention. ✺

All experiences are our personal creations. Personality is the only part of us that cares about how we do something, what we think about any situation. Seeing greener pastures somewhere else is an invitation to look at the present situation from another perspective. We are living the greener grass we saw yesterday. Expressions of "let's change things out there" become "I change myself first." Our growth ripples the spiral of existence. This quest to know ourselves enters a gate *we* negotiate to interact with various people. Each interplay opens another depth of *me*. Relationships are relevant to knowing ourselves, discovering our Essence. The real depth of me cannot be accessed without you. We develop an expanded appreciation of you, of me, for our being ourselves, for being unlike anyone else. We value the differences and honor our unique expression of life while recognizing our present limitations and love OurSelf anyway.

We can read in Genesis that everything is good—the supreme nature of God. "And God saw it was good."[32] Good and bad, right and wrong, past and future—statements that create mental boxes. Our judgments do not change the principle of God/Goodness. Every soldier followed orders based on the judgments of some person or group. Every invader had good reasons for trespassing. We express anger for good reasons. We protect children, we feed the hungry, we love our parents—all because we think we are good people attempting to love our neighbors. We have valid reasons for this conduct. "Surely goodness and mercy shall follow me all the days of my life and I will dwell in the house of the Lord forever."[33]

Our Soul, that aspect of us representing God in our physical life, does not judge—physical reality, actions, thoughts or emotions. Soul creates the universe in which this *I* is living from Its passion, unattached to any outcome. Regardless of beliefs or appearances, accept *Now* as the only experience available for this moment.

> Let personality mind rest.
> I am in the lap of God.
> God never judges, never limits, is always
> present in Love.
> Right now the place of sustenance is here, supported
> by the Heart of the Mother, Earth.
> I can and do have connection with everything.
> I Be in the space of gratitude, responding as I am
> given opportunity.
> Today I serve me in my growth while serving others.
> Any time I do anything for myself I do it to others.
> Any time I do anything for myself I do it for others.
> Planning is unnecessary.
> I am in the energy of BE-ing.
> My doing is generated from this BE.

# 37 Meditation for Being in the Moment

I BEGAN TO USE the following meditation to stimulate momentary awareness. For me, experiencing the body's letting go while being conscious of maintaining the Witness state has taken continued practice. One can achieve an elevated consciousness that notices everything without any need to do anything about what is happening—into no-thing-ness.

❧

Sit comfortably. This can be done with eyes closed or open. Experiment to see which is more comfortable. ❀

Breathe in and out without thinking about the process. ❀

Be aware of the body; if there is tenseness, let it be. ❀

Be present with everything as it is.

Let thoughts come and go like clouds floating through the sky.

Let any emotions be as they are.

Notice any external or internal sounds without identifying them. Ask them to move you into a more detached space. ❀

You might notice your heartbeat. You might notice energy moving in your body. ❀

Let go of needing to do anything about any of this.

Continue to detach as you move into Now, into the space of Being. ❀

Remember to breathe easily, allowing the body to set its own rhythm. ❀

The mind and body are just doing their thing.

Everything is perfect, whatever is happening or not happening. ❀

You might begin to see colors or images; let them be as they are.

Let them move without examining them—even if they decide to stay.

It may seem like imagination—let this be, also. ❀

You might begin to feel tingles, warmth or currents moving through the body.

The body can seem fluid.

Be with any sensations. ❀

You might feel pressure in your head. This, too, is perfect. ❀

If you notice pain anywhere, allow it to be as it is.

Changes may happen all on their own, without your doing anything. Just watch. ❀

Let go of the way you have been. ❀

Let go of all expectations for yourself and others. ❀

Let go of who you think you are. ✹

Let go of needing to do anything, of wanting anything or anyone. ✹

Let go of being. ✹

Let go of God and what that means. ✹

Let go of connection and separation. ✹

Relax ✹ ✹

Be this seeming nothingness. In being nothingness discoveries are made.

In the no-thing-ness feelings are of God

…the body is God,

…the mind and thought is God. ✹ ✹

Decide to embrace God

…your connection to God

…the perfection of God. ✹ ✹

Embrace the nothingness of God

…everything of God—the heart, the Love, the Oneness of All That Is. ✹ ✹

Feel enveloped in any personal awareness of Love. ✹

Begin to be aware of a very deep stillness, ✹ ✹

And at the same time you may feel very alive and very present. ✹

Invite any questions you want to ask or something you want to talk about to surface.

Listen for answers, whether from one of your guides or from your HigherSelf. ❈ ❈

Allow yourself to feel loved; allow yourself to feel cared for, just as you are in this moment. ❈ ❈

Very slowly see if you can expand this feeling to your entire field.

Move into a space of expanded newness

…expanded awareness ❈

…support ❈

…Love. ❈

Invite whatever Is to be present. Be in silence with Self, allowing whatever happens without attachment to any of it. ❈ ❈ ❈ ❈

Bring your awareness to the physical body, noticing any feelings, any sensations. Whatever thoughts pop into mind, welcome them as part of right Now, this Divine moment. ❈ ❈

Breathe from your heart into Earth and back into your heart. ❈ ❈

Take three deep breaths as you return your attention to your body's position and support. Slowly and gently move your fingers, feet, legs. ❈

Begin to stretch. ❈

Open your eyes, becoming totally aware of your surroundings. ❧

# 38  The Fullness of Being

I AM LYING IN BED absorbing Light energies, experiencing tingling body sensations that are intense around my head—pleasant and sensate. There is a feeling of space, of belonging here and there and anywhere individually and all at the same time. And I feel the opposite—of being nowhere at all. Gold colorings appear, changing into a golden city with continually changing architecture—totally fluid, encompassing and distinctly separate. There is no set form.

Realization: There is no set way for anyone to perceive these dimensions. It is all the same regardless of interpretation.

Now I watch the colors change. It makes no difference how it is *seen*. It's the experience that is important. *Feeling* must come first, then pictures can occur. I recognize feelings first as color, then I watch them evolve visually into varying colors, scenes and/or sounds.

My awareness seems to intensify the buzzing feeling in my body. It resounds in my head as a tone. I travel into many dimensions, wherever I ask to go. There is a strong sense that I could go to any one or *the* one just by making the conscious choice. I am free to leave this plane whenever I decide the time is right. I can ask my Spirit to take me out of the earth plane. There would be no trauma, no guilt, no sadness—I can go in joy. My choice is not now. I explore the feelings around this awareness; there is a definite decision to stay. Pictures of happenings that I want to create surface. Spending time with certain people, hugs and cuddles, times of play, times of just being with someone unfolding in the moment. And all of this is totally possible without being physically close to any of them, however, for me, physical contact is an element of joy. Whatever I choose to do is what I will do, without the necessity of prior planning. In the *Being* comes the doing —on many levels.

Parts of this seem strange to my mind, to my consciousness, yet it is so natural. I have a sense of things happening beyond physicality, beyond conscious awareness, beyond mind's knowing. I *know* others are receiving through my experience, through my thoughts of them. My feet feel very warm. Earth's energies are very present. The conduit of love is expanding, horizontally and vertically—beyond Earth, this Universe. The roots that I envisioned days ago are becoming a mass at each end of the column running through the center of my body. The tingles are increasing, my breathing is quickening. I notice the back of my heart is being realigned. I sense projects to complete, to consolidate, to open space for more to be present. My whole life is unfocused. It doesn't make much difference what I do or how I do it. I can do the tasks I have accepted with pleasure. It makes little difference if I stay or go because I am in all spaces, places, things, beings. They are me and I am them—whoever 'they' are or where 'they' may be.

In this time of relaxation, I am comfortable with what is occurring, accepting that all is in order as I move into another aspect of *I Am*. I am a collection of energy vibrations surrounding the *I Am* core called Soul.

There is Essence flowing with every choice you make, every action you take. This happens only in the moment. It cannot be stored up to use on a rainy day or when a certain person is present. Essence is the glue that keeps one in the moment. It is the flow of trans-mutation. It is the movement of attraction between the sperm and the egg. It is the flower and the seed, the fish and water. In life it cannot be divided. Essence is unfoldment, manifestation, enlightenment. It moves mountains. It creates tides. Essence is your heart beating, your lungs expanding and contracting. It is passion. It is life. And It is death. It is miracles.

Life is passion exposing itself in numerous ways through everything you see and every action that occurs—personal countenance expressing. Those who relish living in their past seem to be lagging behind the present evolutionary spiral while others are moving ahead very rapidly. Its optimum development is from inside out allowing the natural flowering of open demonstration. Give it space and time without pushing—let it flow. It's like uncovering a gold mine —some veins seem less than others, yet each aspect is necessary. There is a rhythm set up when you let it come and go freely without analyzing, dissecting or attempting to understand.

Acknowledge yourself enough to know you can express from the core of your Being. Many peripheral expressions crowd in, and while each is valuable within itself, the mixture often becomes implosive. However, it takes all the mud to support the veins of jewels. Each has been a necessary ingredient within the structure. Throw a ball of clay in a stream. Watch it dissolve into its parts while becoming the river. Notice how its incorporation is different from that of a rock or leaf. This is similar to taking responsibility for your life flow. Some things appear as separate parts and some seem to be easily incorporated into your existence. When you become aware that there might be something more valuable within, choose to examine the entire structure to discover the qualities. So often one moves through what seems like debris, discarding this and that without feeling into its entelechy to discover just what the parts do for you. As you delve into the configuration of individual aspects you could discover there is a hidden gold mine with a kernel of truth hidden within the mud.

Everything has value in its inherent core. Time, conditions, experiences, judgments have crowded Essence qualities, changing the definition. Essence qualities are the jewels you are searching for, so go carefully into and through each experience to gather them, while discarding only that which is outdated within the context of your intention. Be grateful for their assistance, regardless of the consequences created. At that time everything was needed to be whatever experience was lived.

There are no requirements to do this or that, to be here or there. Each choice and decision sets in motion whatever comes forth to support individual experiences with the inherent intention of learning how to *Be* Love, no matter what outward expression is present. Love is the ultimate core of everything. It is God in action every second—in sensations, thoughts, emotions and projects. It can seem distorted in various instances, yet, to the individuals involved, expression is an additional place to step into another level of being a GodSelf—God manifesting through this interaction. ✵

We equate the heart as the home of the Soul. When we look into the heart area for the place of the Soul, we find an element of Light. Consider this Light as the nucleus of a cell—any cell of the body. In Oneness there is only One, everything is an element of that One. No matter where we look—our big toe for instance—we can find Soul in any and every cell of our body. It is this one-cell structure that begins all life. Our union with God, sperm with egg, is two parts of One. From this One, Creation takes off. When I, me, the physical, all know Source, these aspects become One Creation, total manifestation. I continually receive messages encouraging us to honor our 'home,' this physical body we inhabit. The messages encourage each of us to be more aware of our physicality, being conscious of how we treat our bodies—food, exercise, cleanliness.

You are created in the image of God. Every molecule of your body is Divinity in form, Essence in operation. Everything you do for your body you do for God. Every time you feed yourself, every time you stroke yourself physically or emotionally or mentally you are doing the same for and to God. It is God loving God, God giving and receiving God. Do you dare encompass the sacred responsibility of One-ness? Your unending search for physical satiation is not only physical; the instinctual longing of your spiritual hunger is satisfied with your opening to Heart Essence. There is so much more to experience—the fullness of your entire fields, interconnecting this Soul.

You are searching for purpose as you re-member your divinity, your true Self. Re-connect to your bodies. Understand that every expression, every experience, is Creation exploring Its *Beingness* through the earthly attribute of choice. How would it be to choose to honor your body as a precious jewel? As you enhance this Self-honoring, you will attract into your daily lives those who have made similar choices rather than those who try to use others to create self-love. Your physical vehicle is the major aspect of your expression on earth—the visual communication device for your Soul's learning and expressing. You have spent lifetimes "hunger[ing] and thirst[ing] after righteousness,"[34] for Oneness. You feed God; you wash God; you admire God in yourself and others—or you don't.

Re-member, bring your power back into your consciousness—your awareness of who is God, the expansiveness of All That Is. Live in companionship with every Creator energy, doing unto others as you do unto yourself with the realization that each of you is ever expanding your perception of everything. As you study, experience and live your expression of God, every minute particle is vibrating with the ascension of its present capabilities. Remember the Oneness of all. Everything reverberates with every expression of any part. What expression do you choose? Consider this carefully and fully live your choice of the moment without excuses.

Realize that every action fulfills a point required for your movement into the next frequency. Your choices can slow down or accelerate the momentum of growth. Awareness is the key, being aware of when you are exhibiting practices that clog the drain, so to speak. It all comes back to momentary response. You are the one steering the ship, guiding the path. You choose when to cut out the rubble, move the debris. No one can do this for another. However, each who travels any path can make it cleaner for the next traveler. You can choose to climb over or detour around the obstacles. Or you may remove the logs, another moves the sticks, another contends with the rocks. In this way you assist in opening a less resistant path. Do you choose to take a machete and move through the jungle? Or do you search for the easy path? Either way you will get where you are going. Honor yourself with all decisions, knowing each is valid for you— just as is every response to life in the moment. ✹

During a group meditation I watched golden energy streams coming from the earth's center. This golden current rose through the EarthStar (the earth connection of every human on the planet) continuing an upward movement in a steady stream. With some, the stream went through the physical body, with others it seemed to detour around. It completely filled the spiritual bodies and flooded the SoulStars. Then each stream circled outward again and moved through the Monads, continuing into All That Is. As this energy reached the Creator Force, another golden stream began a downward spiral through the same points into Shambala, the earth's center. This downward energy rotated constantly, whereas the upward stream was a steady flow. The swirling energy undulated with a continual up-and-down spiraling as well. Its dimensional appearance looked like interlocking infinity signs. I entered the earth, into the depths of Shambala, through the 'other side,' into a place of intense, pale, electric blue light. Then I was taken over my head through layers and systems and universes into a similar Light space. From that place, I looked down on stars and planets, sensing a type of boundary or envelope around these spaces. It seemed as if they were being supported by the membranes that transmitted energy back and forth. They were not stationary, rather they pulsated and moved as if they were one body. Colors swirled. I realized I was seeing the auras of the planets. Astonishing! There was continual acceptance, a total sense of the perfection and beauty within and without. Then as if I were being taken by my hand, I very slowly returned to my present space, becoming aware of my surroundings in the room where the meditation began.

This experience sparked adoration, exaltation, wonder, awe; my physical feelings were being stretched in all ways; my body tingled everywhere. I had immense gratitude for the energies pouring through me. Everyone in the group reported personally empowering experiences during this time. We are powerful *Beings* who can courageously delve into other possibilities or explore any tangent. Some choose to see the forest; some to stand on its edge, perhaps waiting for someone else to join them, while others choose to plunge into its depths. Whatever stand we take, we are expressing our Soul's perfect fullness in Its present design.

# 39 Including and Beyond I

WHATEVER I AM experiencing is not illusionary; it is very present. It floods me within and without, bringing tears of something that I can define as appreciation . . . as acceptance . . . as joy. Maybe this is Love. And yet even with this attempt to share, I realize words are inadequate. This is so personal that no one can give transmissions to another, as we know giving to be. I can *Be* with/in this; you can feel whatever you feel, relate to it as you do—no more or less. In its total presence there is nothing to do, to be, to see, to feel. Nothing is required. In attempting to share this, feelings of inadequacy arise.

What is this space where *I* does not exist? If you and I are one and we are one with every thing, there is no thing. There are these parts of us that want to control, to be something—while there is this existence beyond knowing, a feeling that is even beyond *Is*. Can this be named at all? Aspirations are shed like leaves in the fall. Ideas and dreams become transparent without delineation. Even intentions melt into the stew that we call life until there is no thing distinguishable from another. Even letting go is unnecessary—for there is nothing to release. There is love, there is joy, there is fear. *And* there is a sense of something that can never be defined or put into words—for anything we describe attempts to give delineation, form. And *there is no form*.

Guides, masters, gurus, all of us who have found something

similar (who knows if there is a deeper level?) are present in their Presence to demonstrate possibility—while there is no such thing as possibility—only *Isness*. I recognize the freedom that once terrorized me when I realized there is no thing to do. Now I know *there is no thing else to be or do, no where to go, no thing to get*. There are no words to share the magnitude, the infinite qualities.

I realize I have come full circle into the spiral of existence that defies definition, experience. It makes no difference what I do, who I am with, where I go. There is no thing to do and *every thing Is without any of this being true*.

How do we share this? The phone rings, I engage, I talk, I listen. Everyday events continue. I move from one event to the next with a form of knowing, a feeling, something unexplainable in the flow and rhythm of life here and now. People see me, people ignore me; they want to be touched. I want to eat good food. There are irritants that make my nose stuffy. I get tired if I have only a little sleep. I read. I write. This is life right now. And within or maybe without, there is this peace, this joy of *being*. I share love and physical contact, I soar in orgasmic rapture. And my clothes get dirty and my body needs to be washed and nourished. These things do not change, however my perception of them does. This flow is like a stream, small and contained within banks until it becomes a river and then a sea. Within all of this is freedom beyond my previous knowing or feeling— there is no difference in anything.

I recall twenty years ago reading about a woman sharing her reality after a near-death experience during surgery. She knew and lived a place of total contentment, unattached to outcomes within everyday life—her experiences had proved to her that all is in Divine order. We have spent so much energy and time in attempting to move beyond. *There is no where to go, no thing to get*; no where else but right here. And perhaps there is something else. We don't find out what is around the next curve until we travel through the place where we are now.

There is a whisper. Grace surfaces, encompasses and permeates every particle of everything. It feels to be an intoxicating ecstasy, yet so innocuously silent and penetrating as water seeping through dirt. Words such as peaceful, loving service—as portrayed by Mother Teresa—attempt description. *It* is all-inclusive and there is nothing to include. We attend to our daily activities from a centeredness—without attachment to any outcome, any response or requirement. She did what seemed best in the moment, connected to *being* grace. And so does each of us.

I can hold this space just so long. Then the mind comes in wanting to explain, clarify, longing to know how it will make a difference to humanity when bad things happen. The ego wants to know if you will see any change in me. There is no need for me to slap my hand because my mind says I want you to see me; I can contain such urges. I stop and move into no thing again, realizing that every encounter with this energy, or lack of energy, is a moment of *now* that expands the next moment and the next. Perhaps even this is hogwash.

From today's interchange, awareness happens beyond any consciousness of process. I feel lost and am also found within. I feel so connected to everything and so isolated from expression. Maybe someone notices something different, maybe not. None of this changes what is or isn't, except in my mind. Do the flowers seem brighter? Are auras more visible? Do these perceptions change the way I prepare a meal? My receptivity is altered; my perceptions are clearer. Everything is as it is. And yet nothing is the same. What is illusion and what is fact?

If a moment of passion is exposed as confusion, so be it. Explore it fully as it appears. Hug a tree for as long as you choose and then be something else. Chipmunks play without any concern as they wrestle and tumble. Plants naturally present themselves through the barrier of rocks without struggle. The entelechy of creation. And we think we need to change something? Come on.

Let it be. Accept all as perfection in this moment. From this space love is beyond conditions, no one will ever hurt another. There will be assistance for every creature no matter how many legs it has. Perfection is. Just be with whatever is present—or not. And stay centered—or not. Spirit has placed supportive energy in every life—people, places and groups. I am even more aware of this moment's openness. There is no end to anything. We are a unique journey in process and I am grateful to each of you who is a part of expedition.

There is no where to go and no where to not go. There is nothing to do and no thing to not do. There are no boundaries or directions. Doing or not doing is unnecessary. Being or not being is irrelevant. *What Is is what seems present without attachment to its being this or that—without any need to ever be repeated or felt again.* Stay present. Be so aware that our awareness holds no-thing and every thing.

Forget I am; forget I do—forget all these assumptions we think we understand, want, see and search for. Let go of perfection and imperfection. Feel the no-thing-ness of being. Feel the emptiness of the void. Feel the miracle of freedom. Let's fully live the path of enlightenment in our individual unique Oneness, in the pure state of joyous Love.

# Epilogue

Dear readers, thank you for journeying with me. Many seeds have been sown. Germination may be instantaneous or can take months. Some will grow into ways of life never before experienced—all part of the continual blossoming into the undiscovered. Thanks to all who continue to inspire me with concepts beyond my imaginative powers, be they in physical or ethereal body. With this journey together, our reflections of one another connect our Essences along our unique personal paths. My trust includes God *Being* you and me in the experiences we are—being with us in every way. We are actors in our plays, blossoms on the same tree and fish in the same sea, blessing the profusion of our natural sequences. Inspiration comes from various places; however, the *It* within each of us is God experiencing as *You* and *I*. Be *You* in joy, with gratitude for who you are in the moment, respecting your present characteristics. May each of us enjoy our continuing journey along the path of enlightenment.

The messengers who continually assist me ask to have their voice at the end as well.

Written words to hold interest while the energy of deep truths and meanings surround the writer and reader. Totally understanding the content is unnecessary to reawaken what is already there. Images, be they pictures, statuary or writings, assist in embodying the undiscovered Essence Qualities as one reconnects. Recall our explanation of the act of differentiation—individuality *while at the same time* the holographic whole of Entirety. Those you love mirror aspects of you that are ready to be developed and manifested into your reality, thus enriching your life. So it is with all tangible things, even nature. When you read a book or watch a movie, be conscious of how this material is reflecting you and notice the obscure messages that excite your adventure.

You experience how it is unnecessary to be in their physical presence to be aware of someone. You are together, each reflecting to the other, whether interaction brings love or worry. Be aware of each moment and the contacts you are making. You seek people in whom you sense something you want; peace, serenity, joy and happiness, love, freedom. Whatever its name, each is all the same thing. You want to reawaken these aspects within yourself. Words and exercises keep the mind interested so the interaction between Souls can enhance lives.

Although there is no hierarchy, some of you have discovered a path that others might follow for a while. Whatever the path, it is only a guide. All paths lead to the same place, the God within each individual. Images and experiences are representations of who you are, *for these are all any things have ever been*—mirrors to see YourSelves along your path of enlightenment. ✸

# Sources

*Initiation, Human and Solar*, by Alice Bailey, ISBN 085330-110-7, Lucis Publishing Co. (& other books by Alice Bailey)

*Alice In Wonderland*, by Lewis Carroll (Would you believe there are 36 versions of this classic listed in the *1998-99 Books In Print!*)

*Awakening to Zero Point*, by Gregg Braden, 1997, Radio Bookstore Press

*Bashar: Blueprint For Change*, by Darryl Anka, 1990 by Luana Ewing, ISBN 1-56284-113-0, New Solutions Publishing; *www.bashartapes.com*

*Bringers of the Dawn*, by Barbara J. Marciniak, 1992, ISBN 0-939680-98-x, Bear & Company

*Burgess Bird Book For Children*, by Thornton W. Burgess, 1985, ISBN 08488-0404-x, Ameron Ltd.

*Celebrate The Temporary*, Clyde Reid, 1972, ISBN 0-06-066816-4, Harper & Row

*Conversations with God*, Book 1, 2 & 3, by Neale Diamond Walsh, 1995, ISBN 0-399-14278-9, & 1997, ISBN 1-57174-056-2, Hampton Roads Publishing & 1998, 1-57174-103-8 Hampton Roads Publishing

*Divine Revelation*, by Susan F. Shumsky, 1996, ISBN 0-684-80162-0, Fireside

Dr. Carl Simington is not listed in Books in Print

Earthwatch Institute, 680 Mount Auburn Street, Watertown, MA 02472, 800 776-0188

*Gifts From Eykis,* by Wayne Dyer, 1983, ISBN 0-671-50079-1, Pocket Books

*Gift From The Sea,* by Anne Morrow Lindbergh, 1955, 1975, Random House, Inc.

*Goodbye to Guilt,* by Gerald Jampolsky, 1985, ISBN 0-553-34574-5, Bantam, (and other books by Jampolsky)

*Handbook to Higher Consciousness,* by Ken Keyes, Jr., 1975, ISBN 0-9600686-9-9, DeVorss & Company

*Hands of Life,* by Julie Motz, 1998, ISBN 0-553-10714-3, Bantam Books

*Hands of Light,* by Barbara Ann Brennan, 1988, ISBN 0-553-34539-7, Bantam Books

*Healing the Shame That Binds You,* by John E. Bradshaw, 1988, ISBN 0-932194-86-9, Health Communications, Inc.

*Hidden Mysteries of the Bible,* by Jack Ensign Addington, 1969, ISBN 0-399-55003-8, Putnam Publishing

*How to Love Yourself When You Don't Know How,* by Jacqui Bishop and Mary Grunte, 1992, ISBN 0-88268-131-1, Station Hill Press

*In Each Moment,* Paul Lowe ,edited by Devon Ronner, 1998, ISBN 0-9684109-0-1, Looking Glass Press, Vancouver, BC, Canada

*Is*, Dennis Krum, 720 Seapines Lane, Las Vegas, NV 89107

*I Touch the Earth, the Earth Touches Me*, by Hugh Prather, 1972, ISBN 0-385-05063-1, Doubleday & Company (and other books by Prather)

Inner Focus School of Soul Directed Healing, AlixSandra Parness, D.D., Director, PO Box 82280, Las Vegas, NV 89180-2280, 800 600-8283, email: innerfocus@lvcm.com; www:innerfocus.com

*Iron John:A Book About Men*, Robert Bly, 1990, ISBN 0-201-51720-5, Addison-Wesley Publishers

*Jonathan Livingston Seagull*, by Richard Bach, 1970, Avon Books (& other R. Bach books)

*Joshua*, by Joseph F. Girzone, 1995, ISBN 0-684-81346-7, S & S Trade, (and other books by Girzone)

*Living, Loving and Learning*, by Leo F. Buscaglia, 1985, ISBN 0-449-90181-5, Fawcett (and other books by Buscaglia)

*Love Is letting Go of Fear*, by Gerald Jampolsky, 1995, ISBN 0-89087-344-5, Celestial Arts, (and other books by Jampolsky)

*Love, Medicine and Miracles*, by Bernie Siegel, M.D., 1990, ISBN 0-06091-983-3, Harperernnial Library

*Loving Each Other*, by Leo F. Buscaglia, 1984, ISBN 0-943432-27-8, Slack, Inc.

*Music of the Soul*, by Sidi Shaykh Muhammad al-Famal ar-Rifa'I as-Shadhili, 1994, Sidi Muhammad Press

*Peace Pilgrim*, by some of her friends, 1982, ISBN 0-943734-01-0, Ocean Tree Books

*Psychology, Medicine & Christian Healing,*
by Morton T. Kelsey, 1966, ISBN 0-06-064383-8,
Harper San Francisco

Ram Dass, Hanuman Foundation, Box 478,
Santa Fe, NM 87504; for tapes call 800 248-1008

*Rufus Jones, Master Quaker,* by David Hinshaw,
1951, G P Putnam & Sons

*Seat of the Soul,* Gary Zukav, 1989,
ISBN 0-671-69507-x, Simon & Schuster

*Take Off Your Glasses and See,* by Dr. Jacob Libberman,
1995, ISBN 0-517-88604-9, Crown Publishers (& other
books by Dr. Libberman)

*Talking to Heaven,* by James Van Praagh, 1997,
ISBN 0-525-92468-8, Penguin Group

*The Celestine Prophecy,* by James Redfield, 1993,
ISBN 0-944353-00-2, Satori Publishing

*The Men We Never Knew,* by Daphne Rose Kingma,
1993, ISBN 0-943233-46-1, Conari Press

*The Results Book,* by Wally Minto, 1976,
ISBN 0-89036-11206, Coleman Graphics, Inc.

*The Star-Borne,* by Solara, 1989,
ISBN 1-878246-00-3, Star-Borne Unlimited

*The Thunder of Silence,* by Joel S. Goldsmith, 1961,
ISBN 0-06-063270-4, Harper & Row, (& other books
by Goldsmith)

*Three Magic Words,* by U.S. Anderson, 1954,
ISBN 0-87980-165-4, Thomas Nelson & Sons

*Tying Rocks to Clouds,* by William Elliott, 1996,
ISBN 0-385-48191-8, Image Books Doubleday

*Unconditional Love,* by John Powell, S.J., 1978,
ISBN 0-89505-029-3, Argus Communications

*Vibrational Medicine,* by Richard Gerber, 1988,
ISBN 0-939680-46-7, Bear & Company

*Walk Cheerfully, Friends,* by Seth Bennett Hinshaw,
1978, Merideth-Webb Printing Company

*Way of the Peaceful Warrior,* by Dan Millman, 1985,
ISBN 0-98158-110-6, H. J. Kramer Publishing

*What You Think Of Me Is None Of My Business,*
by Terry Cole-Whittaker, 1988, ISBN 0-515-09479-X,
Jove Books

*Wherever You Go There You Are,* by Jon Kabat-Zinn,
1994, ISBN 0-7868-8099-6, Hyperion

*Wings Of Song,* 1984, ISBN 0-87159-176-6,
Unity Books

*You Can Heal Your Life,* by Louise L. Hay, 1984,
ISBN 0-937611-01-8, Hay House, Inc.

# Notes

1 Anderson, U.S., *Three Magic Words*, Thomas Nelson & Sons, 1994.

2 "Earthwatch", Volume 19, Issue 1, September 1998, page 38.

3 Genesis 1:3.

4 Girzone, Joseph, *Joshua*, S & S Trade Publications, 1995.

5 Massey, Sheilana, *Peace Has No Space for Memories*, Spiral Publishers, 1996.

6 Siegel, Bernie, M.D., *Love, Medicine and Miracles*, Harper Perennial Library, 1990.

7 Symington, Carl, M.D., book no longer in print.

8 Jaffe, Robert T., M.D., 1241 Adams Street, #1132, Saint Helena, CA 94574.

9 Matthew 22:37.

10 Parness, Alixsandra, D.D., Inner Focus School of Soul Directed Healing, PO Box 82280, Las Vegas, NV 89180, 800 600-8283.

11 Bly, Robert, *Iron John: A Book About Men*, Addison-Wesley Publishers, 1990.

12 Millman, Dan, *Way of the Peaceful Warrior*, H. J. Kramer, 1985.

13 Hymnal, *Wings of Song*, page 251.

14 Ram Dass, Hanuman Foundation, Box 478, Santa Fe, NM 87504.

15 Lewis, Carroll, *Alice's Adventures in Wonderland*, Grosset & Dunlap, 1985, page 9.

16 Elliott, William, *Tying Rocks to Clouds*, Image Books Doubleday, 1995, page 69.

17 Massey, Sheilana, *Peace Has No Space for Memories*, Spiral Publishers, 1996, Chapter 5.

18 Lowe, Paul and Ava, c/o Devesh Komaromi, 1413 Argyle, Montreal, QC H3G 1V5.

19 Genesis 1:1.

20 Matthew 7:7.

21 Myss, Caroline, M.D., author of numerous books including *Anatomy of the Spirit*, Harmony Books, 1996.

22 Liberman, Dr. Jacob, *Take Off Your Glasses and See*, Crown Publishers, 1995, page 75.

23 Luke 12:27.

24 Burgess, Thornton W., *The Burgess Bird Book for Children*, Ameron Ltd. 1985.

25 Dillard, Annie, *The Writing Life*, Book-of-the-Month Club edition, 1990, page 72-73.

26 Pilgrim, Friends of Peace, *Peace Pilgrim*, Ocean Tree Books, 1982, page 126.

27 Lindbergh, Anne Murrow, *Gift From the Sea*, Random House, Inc., 1975.

28 Matthew 14:12a.

29 Romans 13:10.

30 Matthew 18:20.

31 Leviticus 19:18.

32 Genesis 1:10.

33 Psalm 23:6.

34 Matthew 5:1.

# ALONG THE PATH TO ENLIGHTENMENT

## SHEILANA MASSEY, D.D.

Published by Lost Coast Press

ISBN 1-882897-55-2     Paper     5½ x 8½     288 Pages

| | Number of Books Ordered ($16.95 per copy) → | | |
|---|---|---|---|
| **LONG THE PATH TO ENLIGHTENMENT**<br>heilana Massey, D.D. | | Subtotal for books: | |
| ❏ Please put me on your book catalog mailing list | | 7.25% sales tax<br>(California residents only): | |
| hipping and Handling Charge: $3.00 U.S.P.S. or $4.50 UPS or Priority Mail;<br>ease add $1,00 for meach additonal book | | Shipping & Handling: | |
| ame | | Total: | |
| ddress | | Daytime Phone<br>(must be included with credit card orders) | |
| ty | State | Zip | Your name as it appears on card: |
| harge to ❏ Visa ❏ MasterCard | | Expiration Date: | |
| ard # | | | |
| uthorized Cardholder Signature | | Thank you for your order | |